# Music Deals

## *A guide to making contracts in the UK popular music industry*

### *Tom Harrison*
*BA, Cert Ed, LLM (Lond)*

Senior Lecturer in Law
Course Leader HND in Music Industry Management
New College Durham

**Harrison Law Publishing 1998**

© TOM HARRISON

ISBN 190188810X

July 1998

Published in Great Britain by
Harrison Law Publishing
53 South Street
Durham City
DH1 4QP

Tel: 0191 3846218
Fax: 0191 3846218

*British Cataloguing-in-Publications Data*
*A catalogue record for this book is available from the British Library*

Printed and bound in Great Britain at Athenaeum Press

*To my wife Glyn with all my love*

# Acknowledgements

The contractual terms in Chapter 3 are reproduced with the kind permission of Butterworths, publishers of The Encyclopaedia of Forms and Precedents. The terms are taken from The Encyclopaedia of Forms and Precedents, Fifth Edition volume 15(1) (1998 Reissue) ENTERTAINMENT AND MEDIA LAW Form 32, Artist's Management Agreement.

I would like to thank Ed Bicknell for reading the manuscript of this book and making constructive and practical suggestions. My thanks go also to John Ellison, Director of the HND Business Studies Programme at New College Durham, who provided legal guidance and support.

Finally I should like to express my sincere thanks to my secretary Moira Page who not only typed the manuscript but typeset the book.

It would be tempting to blame Domino, Sam, Monty and Toto for the mistakes but as usual all errors and omissions remain the responsibility of the author.

The law is stated at 1st July 1998.

T Harrison
Durham
July 1998

# Preface

Having taught law at New College Durham for the last twenty five years (I was recruited as a small child) it was especially challenging three years ago to be made course leader for a Higher National Diploma Course in Music Industry Management. Perhaps my Head of Department had seen me on the Tyneside Metro busking for charity (Action Aid). Whatever the reason, it was certainly an excellent choice of courses, for the students are generally keen and enthusiastic, and quite often realistic about the choices and careers open to them within the Music Industry. Also as an employment/business lawyer I began to appreciate the special significance of the legal professional in the music business and as a result I soon devised and offered a popular module on the course called 'Music Law'.

My experience of teaching the Music Law module led me to believe that there was a demand among musicians, music students and also professional artists and managers for a book which provides a relatively straightforward guide to contracting in the Music Industry.

The aim of the book is to increase awareness of the legal relationship entered into within the business by artists, managers, record and publishing companies. My sincere thanks go out to Ed Bicknell, the Manager of Dire Straits who with 20 years of management experience has provided me with helpful guidance and support. He has constantly reminded me that the legal theory included in the book is often far from what happens in practice. But like me he does believe that artists and managers should be encouraged to appreciate their legal position, to ask questions and to understand the expensive legal advice that they are paying for. In other words the parties to a music deal should at least know what they are letting themselves in for. The purpose of the book is to achieve that aim. We have to look in the main to case law for guidance as to the nature of contractual relationships in the music business. For instance the recent High Court judgment in the Robbie Williams case, reported in June 1998, has provided us with a legal insight to the legal relationship that exists between a manager and a band and I have referred to the decision throughout the book.

For ease of expression the book adopts the practice of using he for 'he or she' and his for 'his or hers'

# Contents

**Legal Terminology**.................................*1*

**Chapter One**
*Introduction*...............................................*5*

**Chapter Two**
*The Music Contract*...................................*25*

**Management Contract Checklist**..................*48*

**Chapter Three**
*Management Agreements*..............................*51*

**Recording Contract Checklist**.....................*84*

**Chapter Four**
*Record Deals*.............................................*87*

**Publishing Contract Checklist**.....................*98*

**Chapter Five**
*Publishing Deals*.......................................*101*

**Index**.........................................................*111*

# Case Law

## Case Law Referred to in the Book

Baron Steven Bentnick v Associated Newspapers Ltd 1997 ... 11

Bettini v Gye 1876 ........................................................ 40

Bolton v Mahadeva 1972 ............................................... 41

Condor v Barron Knights Ltd 1965 ............................. 43,44

Clifford Davis v WEA Records 1975 ...................... 20,37,77

Entertainments Ltd v Great Yarmouth BC 1983 ................. 44

Esso Petroleum v Mardon 1976 ....................................... 33

Hawker Siddley Power Engineering v Rump 1979 .............. 26

Gamerco SA v ICM/Fair Warning (Agency) Ltd 1995 ......... 44

Loftus v Roberts 1902 .................................................... 29

Martin-Smith v. Williams 1998 .. 10,12,21,26,52,63,64,71,72,74

O'Sullivan and Another v Management Agency
and others 1985 ............................................................ 19

Page One Records v Britton 1967 .............................. 22,45

Panayoitou & Others v Sony Music
Entertainment (UK) Ltd 1994 (The George Michael Case) 37,93

Percy Trentham Ltd v Archital Luxfer 1993 ..................... 27

Poussard v Spiers and Pond 1876 ................................... 40

Roberts v Gray 1913 ...................................................... 31

Saunders v Anglia Building Society 1974 ......................... 35

Silvertone v Mountfield and Others 1993 (Stone Roses) ........ 93

Schroeder Music Publishing v Macaulay 1974 ............. 17,105

Taylor v Caldwell 1863 .................................................. 40

Walton v TAC Construction Materials 1981 ...................... 34

Watson v Prager 1991 .................................................... 36

ZTT v Holly Johnson 1993 ....................................... 92,93

Wishart v N A C A B 1990 ............................................. 29

# Legal Terminology

| | |
|---|---|
| *Appeal* | asking a higher appeal court to change the decision of a lower court. |
| *Acceptance* | unconditional agreement to a contractual offer. |
| *Adjudicate* | to settle a legal problem (by a court). |
| *Agent* | a person who is empowered to act on behalf of another. |
| *Appellant* | a person who appeals to a higher court. |
| *Assignment* | legal transfer of a property right such as copyright. |
| *Barrister* | lawyer who has capacity to represent a client as an advocate in any court. |
| *Capacity* | legal ability to enter into a contract. |
| *Civil Action* | a case brought by one person against another alleging a civil wrong such as a breach of contract. |
| *Common Law* | law contained in case decisions e.g. contract law. |
| *Condition* | major contractual term which if broken can lead to contractual termination. |
| *Consideration* | the promises transferred under a contract. |

| | |
|---|---|
| *Consensus ad idem* | meeting of the minds - demonstrating contractual agreement. |
| *Contempt of Court* | failing to obey a court order - which can lead to a fine or imprisonment. |
| *Contract* | a legally enforceable agreement. |
| *Copyright* | a property right which arises automatically without registration in favour of the author of an original musical work. |
| *County Court* | lowest civil court dealing with contract claims of less than £25,000. |
| *Court Order* | giving a judgment. |
| *Damages* | a monetary award by the court. |
| *Defendant* | person who defends a legal action in court. |
| *Discharge of contract* | bringing the contract to an end. |
| *Express Terms* | contractual terms agreed by the parties to the contract. |
| *Fiduciary Duty* | a duty to act in good faith and to disclose matters of interest to another. |
| *Force Majeure* | major force - a clause in a contract to provide for frustrating events. |
| *Frustration* | a radical change in circumstances which will automatically terminate a contract. |
| *High Court* | Civil court which deals with important civil cases. Based in London but goes on circuit to the provinces. |

| | |
|---|---|
| *Implied Terms* | Terms which are implied into contracts by the courts or by statute. |
| *Injunction* | a court order to order or restrain a course of action e.g. a threatened breach of contract. |
| *Interlocutory Injunction* | a temporary injunction. |
| *Judgment* | the decision of a court. |
| *Jurisdiction* | legal powers of a court over a particular type of dispute. |
| *Litigate* | to go to law and take legal action against another in court. |
| *Misrepresentation* | a false statement which induces a contract. |
| *Offer* | an unconditional promise to be legally bound by an acceptance. |
| *Parol Contract* | an oral contract. |
| *Plaintiff* | person who brings an action (sues) another in court. |
| *Repudiatory Breach* | a serious breach of contract entitling the innocent party to terminate the contract. |
| *Rescind* | to annul or cancel a contract. |
| *Restraint of Trade* | the idea that individuals should not be prevented from carrying on their chosen trade or profession. |
| *Solicitor* | a general practitioner of the law who provides legal advice and has a limited right to represent clients in court. |

| | |
|---|---|
| *Statute* | an Act of Parliament. |
| *Terms* | the contractual promises. |
| *Undue Influence* | a relationship where one person has excessive influence over another and can in turn affect a contract's validity. |
| *Warranties* | minor contractual terms which if broken can lead to an award of damages. |

# Chapter One
## Introduction

This book is about making deals in the popular music business. The aim of the book is to explain in relatively straight forward terms the legal significance of the 'music deal' more formally called the music contract. It is by means of contracts that business is conducted in the music industry. Managing, promoting, recording, performing, merchandising, and publishing are all activities which are underpinned by individuals transacting by means of business contracts. It does seem only reasonable that contracting parties, particularly young artists, should be aware of the general content of the deals that they are signing. Pete Townshend made the point very well *"Just because somebody is 20 or 21 and fairly much a novice is no reason not to be taking people properly through agreements that are going to affect them for the rest of their lives"*.

As a law teacher for twenty five years I have taught 'novices'. This book is written for the 'novice'. I appreciate that many creative artists in the popular music industry aren't the least interested in business contracting. But they usually want to be successful and inevitably that means signing deals. Of course when the supply of artists exceeds the demand of record companies the temptation is to sign when given the opportunity and simply accept what is on offer.

Nevertheless there might be room for negotiation, for after all contracts are supposed to reflect a bargain struck by both sides. Even in a take it and leave it situation an artist should understand what's on offer and know what he is letting himself in for. On the other hand people who take risks in business deserve to be fairly rewarded if there is success and most artists appreciate that fact. Long standing successful management relationships such as Mark Knopfler and Ed Bicknell are living proof of that fact. Such relationships survive because of mutual trust and respect between the artist and the manager. They do not depend upon legal ties. Other examples of established management and artist relationships quoted by Ed Bicknell include Eric Clapton and Roger Forrester, Pink Floyd and Steve O'Rourke, Cliff Richard and David Bryce, Genesis and Tony Smith. I would suggest that these relationships have one feature in common which explains their longevity. The artists have the freedom to pursue a creative career with the confidence that their business affairs are in the safe hands of their management. Such confidence doesn't however arise with undertakings and promises, it results from experience. People are judged on their actions rather than their words.

Surely there is no riskier business than the music industry relying on substantial investment with minimal prospects of success. How many deals are allowed to lapse because the artist is not a commercial success? It does make sense therefore to attempt to tie an artist to an exclusive contract for a reasonable term to enable the financial rewards of success to be divided between those who are responsible for it. We will discover however that the courts are prepared to overturn one sided and oppressive contracts in certain circumstances, particularly when the artist is young inexperienced and has received no professional advice. One of our most famous judges Lord Denning once said " *As a matter of common fairness it is not right that the strong should be allowed to put the weak to the wall.* "

There is less sympathy for the established artist who thoughtlessly signs the oppressive deal which could put their livelihood at risk. Why did the Who have the same lawyers as their management, the Kinks allow their managers so much commission, and how could Allen Klein persuade three Beatles in 1969 to sign a one page document which did little more than establish his right to commission? The answer is of course trust! We prefer to see the best in people and creative artists are no different.

There is a legal presumption that the parties to a business deal intend their agreement to have legal consequences and to be contractual. It is this presumption that turns everyday purchases of goods and services such as food and taxi rides into contracts. You should appreciate therefore that business agreements always tend to be contractual and there must be clear evidence to show that the parties to a music agreement did not intend legal relations and so overturn the presumption in favour of a contract. Certainly in the case of a written agreement there would need to be a clear statement that the agreement was not intended to be a contract and that the parties intended to be bound in honour only.

In the field of medicine it is often said that a little knowledge is a dangerous thing and I can see the sense in that statement. I do not however subscribe to that view in relation to the music business. Contracting parties in the music industry should have an appreciation of the respective mutual rights and obligations and such an awareness can, I maintain, help prevent misunderstanding and future conflict from arising. Those artists who create and pay little attention to the business side leaving it to so called professionals sometimes live to regret it. Of course artists should be free to create and managers left to manage. In Ed Bicknell's view, as a manager he would never accept business direction from an artist, but equally neither would he expect to interfere in Mark Knopfler's song writing.

Obviously it is unrealistic to expect an individual to read and digest the terms of a hire purchase contract he has signed or the booking conditions of a package holiday contract. As consumers we can trust to consumer protection law to protect us from unscrupulous traders. The Consumer Credit Act the Sale of Goods Act and the Package Travel Holiday Regulations contain laws to protect the unwary purchaser of goods and services. It's a different story however in the commercial world. While there are exceptions, and we will examine them in this book, the general rule is that in the business world you are bound by what you sign.

The artist who signs a contract is giving his assent to the deal and is taken to be aware of its content. Its all very well for the artist formerly known as Prince to scrawl the word "slave" across his cheek, but he did sign a contract with Warner Bros, and a large corporation won't easily release an artist from a lucrative contract. Independent legal advice is so expensive it makes sense to attempt to appreciate and understand it. Hopefully this book will provide sufficient inspiration and insight to a contracting party to enable him to question and challenge the legal advisor about those aspects of a deal that seem vague, ambiguous or frankly one sided.

I'm constantly asked by my students, why do contracts have to be so long and complex? The answer is of course that while we all yearn for simple straightforward relationships in practice we live complicated lives, and contracts are drafted in the main to reflect our wishes and provide for future occurrences which may or may not materialise. Those knights in the twelfth century who needed to raise money to finance a trip to the Holy Land to participate in the Crusades (a forerunner to the World Cup) did so by means of a dead pledge - a mort gage. They used their lands as security and raised money by means of a mortgage deed redeemable on a contractual date set for redemption. The law of mortgages developed to accommodate the business that mortgagors were transacting. The law of contract has similarly developed over the centuries to accommodate complicated business deals. In the music industry promoters, managers, agents, labels, and artists negotiate what are invariably complicated transactions regulated by a law of contract which is itself necessarily complex.

# Legal Liability

Contracts then are legally enforceable agreements which produce potential legal liabilities. The expression legally enforceable means that the substance of the contract, the contractual terms, may be enforced in a court of law. We will discover that a court could decide that a particular term in a contract is unenforceable because it is too ambiguous or contrary to the public interest. Usually however a failure by either party to a contract to fulfil an obligation contained in a contractual term makes that party potentially liable for breach of contract. The significance of a contractual promise therefore is that if it is broken then the innocent party can seek redress and the party in breach could incur liability in a court of law and be ordered to remedy the breach. Even large corporations have to keep their contractual promises. In 1984 Ray Jackson of Lindisfarne took on EMI for breach of contract claiming that they had failed keep an implied promise to promote his solo career. He won his case in the High Court and secured damages as a remedy.

In practice of course contracts in the music business are entered into between individuals and organisations such as management companies or even large corporations. Such parties do not have equal resources to rely on to pursue a legal action through the courts. The costs of High Court proceedings usually runs into tens of thousands of pounds so a prospective litigant should be very wary before taking legal action. Of course the reasons that individual artists have pursued legal actions in the past are usually that firstly there is something of value worth suing over and secondly they have sufficient financial clout to risk the legal costs of court action. The case-law which provides us with legal guidance resulted from legal claims brought by music artists such as Stone Roses, Joan Armatrading, Holly Johnson, Paul McCartney, Ray Davies, Elton John and George Michael to name but a few. It is said that the costs of George Michael's legal action against Sony ran to £3 million pounds. This sum however is put into perspective when you consider that despite losing the case Virgin were prepared to pay Sony £60 million for George Michael's contract and then offer him a substantial advance to sign. Nevertheless the case illustrates the fact that litigation produces few winners, except of course the lawyers.

In November 1997 the High Court held that Robbie Williams was in breach of a contractual promise in his management agreement to pay commission to his ex manager Nigel Martin-Smith. A figure of £90,000, was ordered to be paid in damages. What happens if a litigant disobeys a court order and refuse to comply with its content? This is called contempt of court and trial judge has wide powers to fine or even imprison a party in contempt. Recently in the North East of England when a young lady refused to obey an undertaking given to the county court to moderate her enthusiastic playing of the latest Whitney Houston release she was imprisoned for contempt of court.

In explaining contempt of court to my students I like to draw on a sixteenth century example of contempt from Wessex Assizes where the accused having "ject une brickbat a le dite justice", (he insulted the judge ), suffered the order of "Son manus dexter ampute pur la contempt". I'm sure that those readers among you who are unfamiliar with this mixture of Norman/Latin nevertheless get the idea, given the importance of the right hand to a musician.While today a person in contempt of court is unlikely to have his right hand chopped off he may be fined or imprisoned.

The majority of contractual disputes are settled following legal advice and compromise. Legal advice in the music business doesn't come cheap but if it leads to the settlement of a dispute then it is money well spent. If the courts are called upon to give a ruling in a contractual dispute, then any undertaking that is given, or order that is made, must be obeyed. In fact only 4% of High Court writs that are served ever lead to a full trial and a court ruling.

Breach of a court order or a promise made to the court in the form of an undertaking can lead to proceedings for contempt of court. In *Baron Steven Bentinck v Associated Newspapers Ltd* 1997 previous libel proceedings had been brought successfully by Baron Bentinck against Nigel Dempster in relation to a reference in his gossip column in the Daily Mail to the Bentinck divorce. The defendants made a payment of £50,000 to settle the proceedings and also undertook not to repeat certain statements, in particular a reference that Baron Bentinck was "mean" to his wife in divorce proceedings. The issue before the High Court was whether this undertaking had been broken when in 1997 Dempster made a further reference to the divorce, stating that the "Baroness received a tax free £5,000 a month settlement - but no lump sum". Judge Walker said that such a statement would be taken as a further imputation of meanness, and held that the undertaking had been broken as a result of ineptitude and negligence rather than deliberate intent. Fines were imposed on Dempster and his employer, but the judge added that had there been a deliberate attempt to break the undertaking a significant jail term could have been imposed.

Contractual agreements then are legally enforceable because they are underpinned by legal sanctions. Non contractual undertakings are not legally binding and are only honoured out of a sense of moral or social obligation. Promises which do not carry the force of law may still be fulfilled however because most of us subscribe to the notion of duty or responsibility and do not want to break our word.

# Writing and Contracts

In the music business you sometimes hear it claimed that a manager and artist are operating their relationship on trust, without the benefit of a contract. This is misleading because the relationship between a manager and an artist necessarily relates to business, will involve an agreement presumed to have been intended to have legal consequences, and will therefore be contractual. In such circumstances there is a contract, although it has not been formally documented. An oral contract is fully legally enforceable; it is just that it is more difficult for the parties to establish the terms relying on oral evidence of agreements and practice. A written contract detailing the terms of the relationship is inevitably much easier to enforce.

In *Martin-Smith v Williams* 1998 it was alleged that an oral agreement between the manager and the band 'Take That', made in the presence of solicitors, to extend the term of the management agreement indefinitely was made subject to contract and so not legally binding. The High Court decided however that as there was no direct evidence that the agreement was intended to be made subject to a written contract it was in fact legally binding, An oral contract to extend the term indefinitely subject to six month's notice and reduce the manager's commission by 5% was enforceable.

Operating without a contract usually means operating without a written contract signed by the parties and containing their fully expressed mutual obligations. Having been employed as a lecturer in employment law at the same college for many years there have been numerous occasions when my teaching colleagues have complained to me that they have never had a contract from their employer. They have of course a contract of employment. What they do not have, or have failed to locate, is a written contract of employment. In fact all employees are entitled to be provided within eight weeks of starting work with a written statement of the main terms and conditions of employment. Without such a statement the contract still exists, it simply becomes more of a challenge to discover its terms from oral and written evidence.

There are sound reasons why a written contract expressing a music agreement is valuable to the respective parties. The first is that the writing will stand as evidence of the existence of the contract should any challenge be made. The second is that the task of reducing what has been agreed into writing is likely to help the parties focus more precisely on the nature and extent of the contractual terms. Statute law actually demands that certain contracts should be made in writing and in some cases in a particular format. A hire purchase contract is strictly regulated by the Consumer Credit Act and is void unless made in writing. For our purpose section 90 of the Copyright Designs and Patents Act 1988 is significant for it requires that a contract to assign a copyright must be made in writing. A music publishing contract which involves the assignment of copyright from the artist to a publishing company therefore has to be in writing.

In the music industry it would be unlikely that a management company, a recording company, or a publishing company would contemplate engaging an artist without relying on a written contract which detailed all the express terms including the mutual obligations of the parties. It is the major challenge of this book to identify and explain the usual terms found in such contracts for the benefit of both parties to them. While such contracts are unique in the sense that they are tailored to suit the needs of a particular artist they will normally follow the same basic format. This is because it is usual for the parties to the contract, on legal advice, to adopt the structure and content of standard form contracts contained in documentary precedents. It is the company which will provide the artist with the draft contract and subject to his status the contract will be presented as the deal or offer, or be subject to the artist's approval and so inevitably further negotiation. We will consider the terms of a standard form management contract in Chapter Three.

# Copyright

Having mentioned the concept of copyright I should make some attempt to explain its significance.

In the music business the product of a creative artist is the song/or recording classified as a form of business property. Under the Copyright Designs and Patents Act 1988 copyright is a property right which exists in, amongst other things, musical works. While there is no legal definition of a musical work it seems that a few original chords will suffice, and for a song a mundane though original lyric will qualify as a literary work. To establish copyright however the original work will have to be fixed in writing or recorded. Being a form of property, copyright confers on the author an exclusive right to exploit the creation in the market place for a considerable period coupled with a range of remedies if the right is infringed. The copyright owner has the exclusive right to reproduce the work, distribute it, periodically perform it and produce derivative works from it. Sometimes the production of the derivative work involves the use of technical skills such as mixing, designing, typesetting and a separate copyright exists in the typographical arrangement of a musical work. Individuals and organisations can of course be licensed to use the musical work in return for fees and royalties.

There is no requirement to register copyright as you would a patent or an original invention, and it will last for the life of the author plus 70 years. One of the unusual features to appreciate about copyright is that it will exist in the original work but in addition copyright exists in what are referred to as derivative works created from the original work. Copyright exists in the original song but also exists in derivative works such as CDs, cassettes, sheet music which in themselves attract copyright. By recording and publishing, musical works are put into a format that enables them to be commercially exploited.

As a form of business property copyright can be transferred (assigned) from one person to another in return for payment (an advance). So by contract a songwriter could in return for an advance, transfer the copyright in his existing and future songs to a publisher. Similarly a band will transfer the copyright in their recordings to a record company under a recording contract in return for a recoupable advance plus royalties.

It is important that the owner of copyright should appreciate that either the full copyright could be transferred or the transfer could relate only to some of the things the owner has the exclusive right to do. Instead of transferring world-wide rights they could be limited to the UK and the transfer could be for a fixed term say for ten years rather than the life of the copyright. This may of course not be negotiable and the size of the advance from the record company will relate to the extent of copyright transferred.

When a lease expires the right to possession of property reverts automatically to the freeholder. Similarly if the copyright in a musical work is transferred for a fixed term, when that term expires the ownership of the copyright reverts to the original owner. In March 1997 the High Court heard that in 1958 Phil Spector assigned the UK copyright in his song "To know him is to love him" to music publishers Warners Music and a licence to Bourne Music for a 28 year term. The court ruled that when that term expired in 1986 the copyright reverted automatically to Phil Spector and no actual transfer was necessary. This meant that Mr Spector was entitled to all the income from the song from 1987. The ownership of the song had reverted to him.

# Freedom of Contract

The philosophy of the free market supports the underlying notion of freedom of contract meaning that as few restrictions as possible should be placed upon the liberty of individuals to make agreements.

A famous 19th century judge Sir George Jessel expressed the idea in the following way in 1875. He said that *"if there is one thing which more than any other public policy requires it is that men of full age and understanding shall have the utmost liberty of contracting and their contracts when entered into freely and voluntarily shall be held sacred and shall be enforced by the courts of justice"*. There still appear to be some compelling reasons for supporting this view.

Firstly, the law of contract is part of private law and this means that the creation and performance of contracts is the responsibility of the parties themselves. Contractual rights and obligations are purely personal and if a contract is broken the only person entitled to redress is the injured party; no one else can sue the contract breaker. Secondly, it is the parties themselves who are best able to judge their own contractual needs and if either party is not happy with the bargain they can always *"walk away from the deal"*. If they are in agreement they should be left alone to make the contract that best suits them and formally incur contractual obligations.

Willing parties to a music contract have the freedom to make the deal that suits them, and as George Michael discovered it is not the role of the courts to intervene and avoid the contract because one party finds it no longer acceptable. In the commercial world the principle caveat emptor (let the buyer beware) still applies. In the absence of fraud or misrepresentation there would be insufficient grounds to negate a contract on the basis of a 'bad bargain'. A contract for a package holiday remains binding even if the holiday maker discovers they are paying a sum in excess of the market price for their two weeks in the Algarve.

What about the young artist/artists who sign an oppressive deal with the management company/publishing company/or recording company. Will the law not provide some assistance if the contract proves to be unfair and onerous. The answer is a qualified yes. The courts may decide that it is in the public interest to protect the artist and declare the contract void. Unfortunately there is no easy answer to the question when will the courts intervene. Obviously George Michael's lawyers felt that in the circumstances of his relationship with Sony the contract he had entered into should be unenforceable. They were proved to be wrong. Perhaps the Court of Appeal or even the European Court may have taken a different view but as there was no appeal we are left with the High Court's decision. It is the case-law that we must turn to provide us with some guidance.

# Restraint of Trade

It is an inevitable consequence of contracting in the music business that an artist will tie himself to a management company, a publishing company or a recording company for a specified term with renewal options. The services he provides will be exclusive. In a management contract there are obvious benefits for both the artist and the management company in the artist tying himself solely to the company for the contractual term. If music contracts conferring exclusive rights are freely entered into then they should be enforced. Lord Reid has said that *"any contract by which a person engages to give his exclusive services to another for a period necessarily involves extensive restriction during that period of the common law right to exercise any lawful activity he chooses in such manner as he thinks best"*. If an artist signs exclusively to one label for a term this necessarily restricts his rights to contract elsewhere.

Normally the doctrine of restraint of trade has no application to exclusive contracts and they require no justification, *"but if contractual restrictions appear to be unnecessary or to be reasonably capable of enforcement in an oppressive manner then they must be justified before they can be enforced."* It seems therefore that if oppressive terms in a contract cannot be justified the courts are prepared to overturn the contract in the public interest. Lord Reid went on to say that *"The public interest requires in the interests both of the public and of the individual that everyone should be free so far as practicable to earn a livelihood and to give the public the fruits of his particular abilities"*. If the effect of an onerous contract is to prevent an individual making a living the courts are prepared to intervene.

In 1974 the House of Lords, the most senior court in England and Wales considered the power of the courts to challenge the validity of a contract on the grounds that it was not in the public interest to enforce a one sided agreement. In the case before it, *Schroeder Music Publishing Co Ltd v Macaulay*, Tony

Macaulay a twenty one year old songwriter had entered into a standard form contract with a music publishing company which turned out to be a nightmare. He had written for a number of singers and had some success with hit singles which included 'Baby, now that I've found you', 'Build me up Buttercup' and 'Love grows where my Rosemary goes'. He applied to the court for a declaration that the publishing agreement was contrary to public policy as being an unreasonable restraint of trade and therefore void. The terms of Macaulay's contract would still be familiar today. The company engaged the exclusive services of the songwriter for a period of five years and under the contract he assigned to the company the full copyright in each musical composition and lyric he produced during that period. Payment was to be made to the songwriter as a general advance recoupable against royalties, and if they exceeded £5,000 the contract was to be automatically extended for a further period of five years. The 50/50 split was standard given it was his first deal, but his songs could be licensed to affiliated publishing houses abroad, and independent audit revealed a major rake off by the overseas companies. While the publishing company had the right to terminate the contract with one month's notice and assign the contract to a third party, there was no corresponding right for the artist. Most significantly for the artist there was no obligation on the company to publish any of the compositions. Effectively the company would act as the final arbiter in deciding whether any of the artist's compositions would be published. There was no obligation on the company to give the compositions proper consideration and even if it was unrealistic to require the publisher to publish there would still have been an obligation to use their best endeavours. The court thought that it was an unreasonable restraint to tie the artist to the company for what would be ten years, during which time his work would become sterile if not published. The copyright in the work would also be assigned to the company and could not be recovered by the artist simply because the company decided not to publish. Certainly the assignment of full copyright to the company for potentially a ten year term with exclusive rights over publication and the unilateral right to assign or terminate the contract indicated a one-sided agreement.

This was a one-sided standard form contract presented by a party enjoying superior bargaining power to an unrepresented weaker party. In such circumstances the courts can intervene to determine whether the bargain is fair and whether the restrictions imposed by the contract are reasonably necessary for the protection of the legitimate interests of the party imposing them. Here the court held that the contract was an unreasonable restraint of trade and therefore void. The restraint of trade doctrine also applies to recording contracts which are considered in Chapter Four. Two notable challenges to one sided recording contracts made by Holly Johnson and the Stone Roses are mentioned in Chapter Four.

# Undue Influence

Another significant factor which may affect the validity of particularly, a management contract is the concept of undue influence. A relationship of undue influence was described many years ago by Lord Chelmsford as occurring *"whenever two persons stand in such a relation that, while it continues, confidence is necessarily reposed by one, and the influence which naturally grows out of that confidence is possessed by the other"*. The relationship of manager and artist is potentially one of undue influence. In *O'Sullivan and Another v Management Agency and Music Ltd and Others* 1985 L J Dunn found that Mr Gilbert O'Sullivan was a young man with no business experience, who *"reposed"* complete trust in his manager the late Mr Mills and entered into a number of contracts with companies in which Mr Mills had a substantial interest, without independent legal advice. In such circumstances the court was entitled to find that the contracts were procured by undue influence and the *"onus of asserting the validity of the contracts to show that they were the free exercise of Mr O'Sullivan's will"* was that of the manager. The court felt that the manager had failed to discharge that burden stressing the failure to encourage

Mr O'Sullivan to seek independent legal advice before contracting.

It is always cause for concern when artists find themselves dealing with an individual who has a number of roles so that there could be conflicting interests. The boxing manager who also promotes the fights could find himself bargaining with himself to extract the best deal for his boxer.

*In Clifford Davis Management Ltd v WEA Records Ltd* 1975 two composer members of the Fleetwood Mac, one of whom was Christine M<sup>c</sup>Vie had signed a publishing deal with their manager's publishing company. Under the contract they transferred the copyright in all their work for up to ten years and in return they were to receive minimal payments. The publisher was obliged to use his best endeavours to publish the work but there was no guarantee. The Court of Appeal found on the basis of bargaining inequality the contract could be set aside at the option of the composers. The factors which the court felt pointed to the inequality were: the overall unfairness of a ten year tie, supported by vague financial rewards; the conflict of interest arising from the manager acting as business advisor to the composers whilst at the same time representing his publishing company's interests in negotiating with them; the absence of any independent legal advice; and their reliance upon the manager who exerted undue influence over them. Lord Denning said that *"one thing is clear from the evidence. The composer had no lawyer and no legal advisors. It seems to me that if the publisher wished to exact such onerous terms or to drive so unconscionable a bargain, he ought to have seen that the composer had independent advice"*.

## Management Agreements, Record Deals and Publishing Contracts

The three most significant contracts that a recording artist in the popular music industry is likely to sign are the Management Agreement the Recording Deal and the Publishing Contract. For this reason I have decided to give special attention to these three contracts in Chapter three, four and five. There you will find some detailed analysis of the usual terms found in such contracts. You should appreciate that when drafting music deals a lawyer will rely heavily on a standard form example and amend the document to suit the needs of the particular parties to the contract These standard contracts are certainly not written in tablets of stone, and it is the job of the music lawyer to negotiate the best deal possible whether his client is the artist, the management company, the record label or the publishing house.

The relationship between a manager (management company) and an artist (a band) must be based upon mutual respect and sustained by an atmosphere of trust and confidence. It is a legal relationship built around a contract and one of the aims of this book is to explain the nature of such a contract in a straightforward manner to assist the manager and the artist in appreciating their mutual rights and obligations under it.

Recent guidance as to the legal nature of the relationship between a manager and a band was provided by the High Court in *Martin-Smith v Williams* 1998. The High Court judge confirmed that a manager in such circumstances owes a fiduciary duty (a duty of good faith) to the artist (the band) and to each individual member, including of course in this case, Robbie Williams. He said that *"I think that the relationship between Mr Martin-Smith (the manager) and Robbie Williams was fiduciary because of the degree of control over his affairs which Robbie Williams conferred on Mr Martin-Smith, the element of agency and the need for continued trust and confidence between them. The same relationship extended of course between Mr Martin-Smith and the other members of the group"*.

One piece of advice from the outset however! A management contract cannot sustain the relationship if there is a breakdown in trust and confidence. A management contract is like a marriage contract in that if the relationship is irretrievably broken-down the marriage is unlikely to survive no matter how well the contract was originally drafted. In the event of a breakdown in a management relationship however it is to the management agreement that we must turn to determine the respective rights and duties of the parties to it. The terms of an enforceable management agreement which express the intention of the parties will be the vehicle used to sort out the legal position following breakdown.

Hopefully this book will provide more than a guide to legal rights on relationship breakdown. Certainly the courts will not enforce a management contract where trust and confidence is broken down. In *Page One Records Ltd v Britton* 1968 there was a clear provision in the management contract between Larry Page and the Troggs to the effect that the band would not *"engage any other person, firm or corporation to act as manager or agent for "the Troggs" nor act themselves in such capacity"*. The court refused the manager an injunction to enforce this negative stipulation on the grounds that the Troggs would then be forced to retain the services of the manager, someone in who they had lost mutual trust. While it would be far fetched in the extreme to expect a new or established artist to analyse the individual terms of a management contract or a recording deal before signing it there should be legal advisors available to indicate the controversial terms. My book is an attempt to assist both managers and artists to appreciate the content of a standard form management, recording and publishing agreements, to ask the right questions and to benefit fully from the costly legal advice they are given.

In a contractual relationship there has to a meeting of the minds of both sides. Lawyers refer to this understanding *as consensus ad idem*. It can only occur if the parties to the deal know what they are letting themselves in for. Once the deal is signed and the contract entered into the relationship will commence. Potentially it may last for many years. It is this contract which will regulate the relationship and hopefully this book will serve as a guide to understanding the nature of the contractual terms as they are put into effect. Frankly some terms in recording, management and publishing contracts are never addressed or even considered, for instance the right of the manager or company to suspend the contract. Other terms will inevitably be interpreted and applied, such as those dealing with the financial positions of the parties. The legal advisor of an established artist will insist on the inclusion of contractual terms to cover every conceivable dispute. The prospective manager of an established artist will of course be more willing to negotiate contractual terms.

You should appreciate of course that the music industry is highly diverse. It operates through organisations such as multinational corporations and small independent labels and individuals. These parties find themselves entering into a multitude of transactions, the nature and scale of which reflects the richness of the industry's commercial and artistic fabric.

These transactions are all contractual in nature and cover a range of activities: Management; Recording; Touring; Publishing; Merchandising; Distribution; Manufacturing; Services; Sponsorship.

While in a book of this nature it would not be possible to carry out a detailed analysis of the terms found in each of those contractual relationships the same basic principles of law apply to their formation, operation and termination. Chapter Two of the book is devoted to a consideration of the basic principles of contract law relevant to music contracting. For the majority of artists the three core contracts are the management, recording and publishing deals. I have devoted Chapter Three to an examination of the standard management contract. Chapter Four contains an analysis of the standard terms found in recording contracts and Chapter Five publishing contracts. Anyone who signs a deal which affects their future livelihood should have some notion of what they are signing. Hopefully the checklist of relevant questions and the explanations of legal terminology will go some way to assist the parties to a music deal in understanding their legal rights and obligations arising under it.

There is of course an added complication with music deals in the popular music industry. Quite often the contract is made with a record or management company and a band composed of individual members. In Ed Bicknell's view the most likely source of legal conflict occurs not with management or the record company, but when there is a relationship breakdown between the individual band members. Such break ups are rarely amicable and the legal and financial wrangle that occurs can be very costly and sometimes ends in litigation. The High Court decision in *Martin-Smith v Williams* 1998 is about a manager suing an artist for commission due following the relationship breakdown between Robbie Williams and the rest of the members of 'Take That'.

# Chapter Two
## The Music Contract

Contracting parties in the music business should be aware of the basic elements of a binding contract. It is also useful to appreciate that in certain circumstances music contracts may be declared invalid, and also to understand the various options available if a contractual term is broken.

To form a contract certain requirements must be met. These are that capable parties have entered into an agreement intending to bind themselves legally and having exchanged something of value.

## The Agreement

A contract cannot be created without the parties reaching an agreement. The idea of agreement is therefore central to an understanding of the law of contract. There are two basic questions which arise in respect of all transactions whether they relate to management, promotions, recording or merchandising. They are, firstly, whether a legally enforceable agreement has been made, and secondly, what are the terms upon which it is based. The answer to the second question reveals the specific obligations each party owes towards the other. These obligations are of fundamental importance to them both. It is only by identifying the content and extent of their mutual undertakings that the parties are able to know when they have discharged their responsibilities under the contract. The two questions are of course very closely connected because it is through the process of reaching their agreement that the parties will fix the terms that regulate their contract. In other words agreements are usually undertakings to do specific things and these specific things are the terms of the contract.

The fundamental undertakings in a management contract are the obligations to manage and promote the interests of the artist in return for the payment of commission on earnings. Most people can rely on instinct or common sense to assess whether they have an agreement or not, but for legal purposes it is not sufficient to rely upon subjective judgments to decide such significant events. If a disputed agreement comes before a court, obviously the courts cannot get inside the minds of the parties to discover their actual intentions. At best all that can be achieved is to look at the way the parties have conducted themselves, examining what they have said and what they have done, in order decide the matter on the basis of what a reasonable person would assume their intentions to be. That is why it is often necessary to hear a great deal of evidence in a contractual claim to determine what the parties actually agreed. The evidence in *Martin-Smith v Williams* 1998 suggested that 'Take That' and their manager did in fact reach an oral agreement in the presence of lawyers to extend the contractual terms of their management contract *"indefinitely"* and also reduce his commission by 5%. The judge said that *"The extension of the Management Agreement was something which was capable of being the subject of an oral agreement. In my view if parties reach accord by means of offer and acceptance then they should be treated as contractually bound to each other unless it is shown that such accord is subject to a condition"*.

A written contract is of course primary evidence as to the actual agreement but there have been cases where the courts have admitted conflicting oral terms to reflect the true intentions of the parties.

In *Hawker Siddeley Power Engineering Ltd. v. Rump* 1979 the complainant was employed as a heavy goods vehicle driver in 1973 and signed a contract of employment which stated that he would be liable to travel all over the country. This obligation was confirmed in a later statement of terms of employment issued in 1976 and signed by the employee. In fact the complainant had made it clear when he took the job that because of his wife's illness he would not travel outside the south of England and that had been orally agreed by a manager when he signed the contract. When finally in 1978 the complainant refused to obey an instruction to travel to Scotland and this led to his dismissal, one issue before the EAT was whether he was contractually obliged to do so. The EAT held that the promise to work only in the south was an oral contractual term. Here *"there was a direct promise by the employers which must have become part of the contract of employment because it was following upon the promise that the employee signed the contract"*. Even the subsequent written statement which included a mobility clause signed by the employer was insufficient to exclude the oral term previously agreed. Here the employee *"had no notice that the oral term he had secured was going to form no part of his new contract. The mere putting in front of him a document and invitation for him to sign it could not be held to be a variation by agreement so as to exclude the important oral term which he had previously secured. Rather if there was a variation at all to the contract, it was a unilateral variation which was not binding upon the employee"*.

The conduct of the parties may be crucial evidence of the existence of a contract. The fact that an individual carries out the role of manager in relation to an artist indicates that there is a management contract.

The Court of Appeal reviewed the question of contractual formation in *G Percy Trentham Ltd. v. Archital Luxfer Ltd.* 1993. The plaintiffs were the main contractors engaged in a building contract, and they had negotiated with the defendants a sub-contract under which the defendants were to supply and fit architectural furniture such as doors and windows. The sub-contract was satisfactorily performed, but a dispute arose when the plaintiffs, who were obliged to make a penalty payment under the main contract, sought a contribution from the defendants. The defendant's response was that no contract had ever been concluded between the parties. Telephone calls had been made and letters exchanged but no discernible offer and acceptance could be identified. As a result it was not possible to determine whose standard terms of trading applied to the agreement.

The Court of Appeal held that a contract had been made between the parties. In carrying out the work the defendants had agreed to an offer from the plaintiffs.The court took the view that the test to determine whether a contract has been formed is an objective one, and in this case one should look to *"the reasonable expectations of sensible businessmen"* rather than the *"subjective and unexpressed mental reservations of the parties."* Although the usual mechanism of contractual formation is offer and acceptance in some circumstances this is not necessary. The instant case was an example, which concerned *"a contract alleged to have come into existence during and as a result of performance."* The contract was an executed one (i.e. it had been carried out) making it very difficult to argue lack of intention to create legal relations, or invalidity based upon uncertainty of terms. *"If a contract comes into existence during and as a result of performance of the transaction, it will frequently be possible to hold that the contract impliedly and retrospectively covers pre-contractual performance."*

# Offer and Acceptance

Agreements are composed of two elements, the offer and acceptance. If the acceptance is conditional then this constitutes a counter offer which is capable of acceptance or rejection. If in response to the offer of a recording contract the artist accepts subject to conditions then there is no contract unless the record company agrees to those conditions without qualification. If the offer itself is made subject to conditions such as *"passing a medical examination"* there is no contract until that condition is satisfied.

In *Wishart v. National Association of Citizens Advice Bureaux Ltd.* 1990 The Court of Appeal considered a case where the plaintiff had been offered the post of information officer "subject to satisfactory references" and then when the employer discovered his past attendance record withdrew the job offer. The issue before the Court of Appeal was whether the employer's decision to treat the references as unsatisfactory could be viewed objectively and tested by the standard of the reasonable person in the position of the employer. In fact the court decided that unlike medical opinion as to the employee's fitness which could be tested objectively, there was no obligation in law on the employer other than to decide in good faith whether the references were satisfactory. *"The natural reading of a communication, the purpose of which is to tell the prospective employee that part of the decision on whether he is firmly offered the post has yet to be made, is that the employer is reserving the right to make up his own mind when the references have been received and studied."*

For a genuine agreement there should be certainty of terms. The courts will always endeavour to find certainty so that the contract is able to survive wherever possible but if a term is obscure or meaningless then it will fail. This may not prove fatal to the contract if the term constitutes only a minor part of the overall obligations, but where the term is central to the functioning of the contract, uncertainty as to its meaning will defeat the contract as a whole. The following case illustrates the position.

In *Loftus v. Roberts* 1902 an agreement provided for the appointment of an actress by another person at a *"West End salary to be mutually agreed between us."* Subsequently the parties were unable to arrive at a salary which satisfied them both. The court held that the contract must fail. Even if it were possible to assess a suitable salary by reference to West End rates of pay, the court could not impose such a figure since the parties had already stated that it had to be mutually agreed, something they had been unable to achieve. What they had was an agreement to agree at a further date. The contract failed.

Contractual offers will not lie on the table for ever and will lapse if subject to a time limit and that time expires. If there is no time limit for the publishing deal then the offer will lapse after a reasonable length of time. It does seem reasonable commercial practice that an offer of management or recording will lapse after a number of days or possibly weeks but certainly not months. Knowing that the offer of a record or publishing deal will lapse or may be withdrawn often convinces young artists that they should sign and worry about the consequences later. There are hundreds of unsigned bands to whom the record company can turn if the young artists seem uncooperative. The fact that a counter offer will destroy the original offer makes it less likely that an unsigned band will bargain keenly. The thought that by bargaining keenly the original offer could be destroyed is very concerning for the artist who usually wants to sign the deal despite its one sided nature. The economist explains it in terms of supply and demand. In most contracts of employment the employee usually takes what's on offer but its a different story if the prospective employee has some status. To attract the right person an employer like a manager or a record company may be willing to negotiate, to bargain and strike a genuine deal.

# Consideration

Unlike other legal systems English law requires that contractual agreements must be supported by the element of consideration. It is not necessary in a book of this nature to dwell upon this element, merely to say that it constitutes the value that is transferred by the parties under the contract, the quid pro quo. It could be tangible in the form of money for goods but in the commercial world it is usually intangible and consists of the parties undertakings. In a recording contract the promise to write and perform by the artist is supported by the promise of recoupable advances and royalties by the recording company. In a management contract the promise to advance the artist's professional career and secure suitable work is supported by the promise of a percentage on earnings.

# Capacity

Contracting parties must have contractual capacity. This means that they have legal authority to enter into the contract and full contractual capacity is not achieved until an individual reaches the age of majority, which since 1970 is now eighteen years of age. Anyone under eighteen is a minor and the law has always sought to protect minors from the consequences of transactions detrimental to themselves. The aim has been to provide them with some protection from their lack of commercial experience, whilst at the same time recognising circumstances where it is appropriate that they should be fully accountable for the agreements that they make. Contracts with minors in the music business will be enforceable but only if they are substantially for the minor's benefit and involve some element of education or training. The educational element is given a broad interpretation so that *in Roberts v. Gray* 1913 the defendant, a minor, with a view to becoming a professional billiards player, had entered an agreement with the plaintiff, himself a leading professional, to accompany the plaintiff on a world tour. The plaintiff spent time and money organising the tour, but following a dispute the defendant refused to go. The plaintiff sought damages of £6000 for breach of contract. The Court of Appeal held that the contract was for the defendant's benefit, being in the nature of a course of instruction in the game of billiards. The plaintiff was awarded £1500 damages.

Usually minor's contracts are counter signed by a parent or guardian or guarantor.

It is of course possible to contract with an artificial legal person, a registered company. The management company or record company has contractual capacity linked to its commercial objects. Provided it acts within its powers it will be always legally bound by its contracts, and it may be bound by contracts made outside its commercial powers.

# Invalid Contracts

You should be aware that circumstances sometimes arise which affect the validity of a contract. The primary aim of contracting parties is to reach an agreement where there is said to be *consensus ad idem* - a meeting of the minds. If there is evidence to suggest that there was no genuine consent to the bargain then the courts may be prepared to invalidate the contract by declaring it void and of no legal effect. Alternatively the contract could be declared voidable so entitling the innocent party to escape from the contract if he or she wishes to do so. The factors that a court takes account of in deciding whether there has been true consent to the bargain include misrepresentation, fraud, mistake, duress and undue influence. In laymans terms false inducements, genuine misunderstandings, trickery, coercion and bargaining inequality may all have impact upon the validity of a contract to manage, record, or publish an artist.

# Misrepresentation

False statements made during the contracting process may provide the injured party with a legal remedy if she subsequently contracts relying upon them. A misrepresentation is a false statement of fact which induces a contract. Selling an independent record label to an established artist could involve using superlatives which are statements of opinion and so not actionable if they prove to be false. To say that the label is the fastest growing in UK in 1998 is a statement of fact which if false and relied upon by the artist could constitute misrepresentation. A recording contract signed as a result could be voidable in favour of the injured party.

With misrepresentation we are concerned with false statements made during the contracting process which induce the contract but do not become part of it. A prime example would be exaggerating the size, or turnover of an organisation when promoting it to a prospective artist.

Obviously this is even more crucial in the sale of a business as so in *Esso Petroleum v Mardon* 1976 the Court of Appeal found there was a negligent misrepresentation when the experienced seller of a filling station made a forecast as to the expected turnover of the garage to the purchaser based on previous years figures and it was grossly inadequate. Lord Denning MR's comments are helpful. *"It was a forecast made by a party, Esso who had special knowledge and skill. It was the yardstick by which they measured the worth of a filling station. They knew the facts. They knew the traffic in the town. They knew the throughput of a comparable station. They had much experience and expertise at their disposal. They were in a much better position than Mr. Mardon to make a forecast. It seems to me that if such a person makes a forecast – intending that the other should act on it and he does act on it – it can well be interpreted as a warranty that the forecast is sound and reliable in this sense that they made it with reasonable care and skill. That warranty was broken. Most negligently Esso made a fatal error in the forecast they stated to Mr. Mardon, and on which he took the tenancy. For this they are made liable in damages."*

Some contracts are classified as uberrimae fidei *"of utmost good faith"* and this means that the contracting parties are legally bound to disclose matters of interest to each other. A partnership contract would fall into this category so there is an obligation on the prospective partners to reveal their past and present financial status. The failure of one partner to reveal that he had been a bankrupt could make the partnership contract void. A contract of employment would not fall into this category or a contract to engage an artist. As there is no obligation to volunteer information it is in the parties interests to carefully question through interviews and application forms.

A good example is provided in the field of employment law by *Walton v TAC Constructions Materials Ltd* 1981 where the complainant was dismissed when after working for thirteen and half months the employer discovered that he was a heroin addict. During a medical inspection prior to employment the employee had answered "none" when asked to give details of serious illnesses and failed to reveal that he was injecting himself with heroin. The industrial tribunal decided that it was fair to dismiss him because of the deception. They also confirmed however that *"it could not be said that there is any duty on the employee in the ordinary case, though there may be exceptions, to volunteer information about himself otherwise than in response to a direct question"*.

# Mistake

The courts have always been reticent about treating mistake as a ground for the avoidance of contractual liabilities. A contract remains valid despite it proving to be economically disadvantageous to one of the parties perhaps due to their mistaken belief. Provided the parties have made their deal openly and voluntarily the courts will enforce it. If someone buys a car privately and subsequently finds they have paid well above the market price, or the car is much heavier on petrol than anticipated, or is simply not a very good vehicle, the law does not give them any remedy against the seller. If the band who have signed the record deal prove not to be as creative or inspirational as was first envisaged then it may prove to be a mistake to have signed them but the contract remains valid and enforceable. This is simply an error of judgment that will have no impact on contractual liabilities.

In 1974 the highest court in the land the House of Lords considered the case of a 78 year old widow who was induced by fraud to sign away her property. The reason she had not read the deed of transfer before signing it was that her glasses were broken. The court was not sympathetic! She had been careless and the courts are reluctant to override the rule that you are bound by what you sign. The lesson from *Saunders v Anglia Building Society* is that it is very rare for the courts to accept a plea that a document was signed by mistake and should not therefore be legally binding.

# Duress and Undue Influence

The coercion of a person into making a contract by means of actual or threatened violence to them is referred to as duress and if it can be proved the contract is treated not surprisingly as void and of no legal effect. If it can be established that the contract was signed under death threats or even *"sign here or else"* then the contract is void. A more subtle form of improper pressure is called undue influence and if it arises the innocent party has the option of bringing the contract to an end. In certain relationships a presumption of undue influence arises for example in what is called fiduciary relationships or where the person is in a position of dominance over the other. Parent and child, solicitor and client, doctor and patient and trustee and beneficiary, bankers and client are classic illustrations.

As we have seen, in the music business managers, record companies and publishing companies are regarded as being in a dominant position in relation to artists and consequently the relationship is presumed to be one of undue influence. The dominant party who attempts to enforce a transaction entered into in such a relationship must overturn the presumption of undue influence by showing he has not abused his position in any way. Evidence that the innocent party has taken independent legal advice will go a long way to achieving this and saving the contract.

# Restraint of Trade

Although contracts are part of private law, this does not make contracting the exclusive domain of the parties themselves, granting them freedom to make whatever type of contract they choose. Certain types of contract may be regarded as illegal and void on the basis that in the view of the courts they are contrary to public policy. Obviously a contract entered into for the purpose of committing an illegal act will be void as would a contract tainted with illegality. A contract of employment is void if the employer and employee fraudulently agree not to make deductions of income tax and National Insurance.

One aspect of illegality which is sometimes pleaded in relation to music contracts is the claim that a management contract or a publishing contract should be declared void as an unreasonable restraint of trade. A contract in restraint of trade is one which restricts the future freedom of one of the parties to carry on their chosen trade or profession with others who are not parties to the contract. Inevitably music contracts tend to be exclusive but they can only be successfully challenged if they are regarded as unreasonable from the point of view of the parties and the public interest. In the music industry a balance has to be struck between the commercial interest of the company and the rights of the artist to exploit his talent. A good example of challenge to a management contract on the basis of restraint of trade is provided from the world of boxing.

This was the position in *Watson v. Prager* 1991. The plaintiff, a boxer, entered into a contract in 1987 with the defendant, better known as the boxing promoter, Mickey Duff. The contract provided for the defendant to act as the plaintiff's manager for three years. The defendant had an option to extend the period for a further three years if the plaintiff won a title. He did so in 1987, taking the Commonwealth Middleweight championship. The defendant then exercised his option to extend the management contract. The plaintiff's claim was that the extended contract was an unreasonable restraint, because the defendant in his capacity as a promoter could arrange a fight for the plaintiff, and in his capacity as a personal manager require the plaintiff to take part in it. This was a conflict of interest, since the defendant's responsibility towards the career interests of the plaintiff could conflict with his personal financial interest in a promotion. The court agreed. The test for a restraint is what could happen within the scope of it. The fact that under this contract a conflict had not yet occurred, and indeed might never occur, was not relevant to the validity of the restraint.

The kind of tie occurring in *Watson v. Prager* is standard practice in the music industry where recording contracts between musicians and their recording companies generally bind the parties to each other for many years, frequently resulting in well publicised disputes when companies refuse to release their artists from the recording deal that had been signed. The musicians argue that these ties restrict their artistic freedom or complain that their companies do not sufficiently promote them. Lawyers for the musicians rely on the claim that long tie clauses are an unreasonable restraint and that the agreements containing them are frequently tainted by undue influence, the argument used in *Clifford Davis v. WEA* 1975 considered earlier in Chapter One.

In these cases a crucial question will be whether the agreement has been signed after taking independent specialist advice. If it has a court will be far less likely to declare the agreement invalid. Such was the position in *Panayoitou v. Sony Music Entertainment (UK) Ltd*. 1994 where George Michael unsuccessfully sought to extricate himself from a 15 year deal with Sony. His original contract with the company gave him the opportunity to renegotiate it, and he had used this option to secure superior terms for himself. These terms were renegotiated for him by specialist lawyers. A clause in the renegotiated contract said, *"I am not a minor and I have taken legal advice in relation to this agreement prior to entering into the same."* This evidence, the court felt, supported the view that the contract should be upheld.

One of the most controvertial terms found in management contracts relates to the managers rights to commission following the termination of the contract on the artists earnings from deals negotiated during the contractual term. Such clauses may be for a fixed term of years following the contractual termination or in rare cases they could require commission in perpetuity. Even if the commission is payable at a reduced rate, commission in perpetuity seems excessive. Such a term was the subject of litigation in 1988 when Joan Armatrading sued her former manager Mike Stone. The claim was that the commission in perpetuity clause constituted a restraint of trade making the contract she signed in 1976 without independent legal advice unnecessarily oppressive. The argument was that the artist could not pursue her career with new management if she had still to account to her previous manager for a proportion of her earnings. The High Court held that while *"every case needs to be examined on its merits"* the original management contract and consequently the commission in perpetuity clause was invalid.

# Contract Terms

Students often ask me, particularly in the field of employment law, why do we need to have formalised contracts which by their very nature are long and complex and frankly daunting. The vast majority of terms within contracts are never addressed or even considered so why are they included. The answer is of course that the parties to a music contract insist on their inclusion to provide for the position of the parties in the event of a future occurrence which may or may not happen. The idea is to cover all eventualities. Contracts are structured according to the status of the parties and it could even be the lawyers for the artist who insist on the inclusion of terms to protect their client against every conceivable dispute.

The terms of a contract are the obligations and undertakings owed by the parties to each other under it. All contracts contain terms. In transactions involving large sums of money, or where the agreement is of a complex or technical nature, the terms are likely to be numerous and detailed. By inserting terms into the contract the parties will be trying to clarify their mutual obligations. They will be attempting to define the nature and scope of the contract, and will try to anticipate eventualities which may possibly emerge after the contract has been made but before it has been carried out. Thus they will make provision for such contingencies as contractual terms. In the simplest contracts terms will be single promises made by each party to the other. In more complex agreements however the contract may run into many pages of detailed obligations. Consider the numerous terms found in standard recording, management and publishing contracts in Chapter Three and Five

# The Classification of Terms

The terms of a contract vary in importance. Sometimes the contract itself will say how much importance is attached to a certain term, while in other cases it may be left to the court to decide the question because the parties to the contract have not made it clear. The value that is attached to each term is of great significance because it determines what the consequences will be if the particular term is broken.

Major terms are called *conditions*. A condition is a term which is said to go to the root of the contract, and where performance is essential to the contract. If it is broken the innocent party has the right to treat the contract as repudiated and to refuse to perform his or her obligations under it. In addition the injured party may sue for damages.

Minor terms are called *warranties*. They are terms which are said to be collateral to the main purpose of the contract. In consequence, if a warranty is broken the contract still stands, and the innocent party does not have the right to treat the contract as being at an end, merely the right to damages.

Where breach of a condition occurs the injured party is not bound to repudiate the contract. As an alternative the injured party can elect to treat the contract as subsisting, treating the breach of condition as if it were a warranty, and only damages will be available. There may be sound commercial reasons for treating a breach of condition as one of warranty, and letting the contract stand. The innocent party may realise that if the contract is repudiated it will be difficult to negotiate an alternative deal.

Two classic cases from the nineteenth century illuminate the distinction between important terms (conditions) and less important terms (warranties) in a contract. In *Bettini v. Gye* 1876 the plaintiff, an opera singer agreed in writing to sing in various concerts and operas over a period of three and a half months, and to be present at rehearsals for at least six days before the engagements were due to begin. Due to illness he arrived with only two days of rehearsals left, and as a result the defendant terminated the agreement. Looking at the contract as a whole, the court decided that the rehearsal clause was not a condition, but merely a warranty, for which damages alone was the remedy. The contract had been wrongfully terminated and the plaintiff could counter-claim for damages.

In *Poussard v. Spiers and Pond* 1876 an opera singer was unable to take part in the first week of performances due to illness. In the meantime the management had engaged a substitute and refused the original singer the part when she arrived. They were held to be entitled to do so, for her non-attendance at the performances was a breach of a vital term of the contract.

Those terms which have been expressly agreed by the parties either orally or in writing are called express terms. You should appreciate however that terms may also be implied into contracts through the mechanisms of Acts of Parliament or by the action of the courts. In consumer contracts, terms are implied to protect the purchaser of goods and services and in employment to impose duties on the employer and the employee. Implied terms are however less likely in the commercial world where the parties to the contract are responsible for agreeing their respective rights and obligations.

# Performance

Once a contract has been entered into it becomes the responsibility of the parties to carry out their obligations under it. The music contract could involve an ongoing publishing deal or relate to a single musical performance. In either case the onus on the contracting parties is to provide precise complete performance of the contract. The general rule is that in a *"contract to do work for a lump sum, until the work is completed, the price of it cannot be recovered"*. Inevitably the law of contract provides us with exceptions to this rule and one of relevance to the music business is the doctrine of substantial performance.

If a party to a contract has substantially performed his contractual obligations subject only to minor defects, the courts have recognised that it would be unjust to prevent him recovering any of the contractual price. Therefore under this exception the contractual price would be recoverable, less of course a sum representing the value of the defects. It must be stressed that the exception will only operate where the defects are of a trifling nature, an issue determined by considering not only the character of the defects but also the cost of rectifying them in relation to the total contract price.

A claim of substantial performance of the contract was made *in Bolton v. Mahadeva* 1972. The plaintiff, a heating contractor, had agreed to install a central heating system in the defendant's house for £560. On completion of the work the system proved to be so defective that it would cost £174 to repair. The defendant refused to pay the plaintiff any of the cost of the work and the plaintiff sued. The County Court accepted the plaintiff's claim of substantial performance and awarded him the cost of the work less the cost of the repair. On appeal however, the Court of Appeal held that in the circumstances the plaintiff had not substantially performed the contract and he was not therefore entitled to recover any of the cost of the work. The substantial performance plea would not succeed where there were numerous defects requiring a relatively high cost of repair.

It is of course difficult to ascertain in any given case whether incomplete performance of a contract constitutes substantial performance but the golden rule seems to be that only a minor failure of performance is acceptable. The argument of substantial performance could be used to obtain a proportion of payments for the live performance or recording where the artist does not give full value.

# Agreement

Contracts are agreements and contracting parties can agree to waive their rights and obligations under them and so discharge themselves from the contract. To be an effective waiver the second agreement must be a contract, the consideration for which in the exchange of promises not to enforce the original contract. When the football manager mutually agrees to terminate his contract with the club there is usually a financial consideration and this would be the case with an artist and manager. It is even possible in the music business for a management team to agree to cancel their management contract with an artist and for another management company to take over in return for a percentage share of the future earnings under the new contract. Artists such as Hazel O'Connor discovered to their cost that if previous managers continue to take bites from the cake the artist may only be left with the crumbs. I should stress that this practice is very rare and unlikely to occur in practice.

# Frustration

A contract may be regarded as frustrated and so terminated if because of a change in circumstances, performance of the obligations under it becomes radically different from the performance envisaged by the parties to the contract.

In *Taylor v Caldwell* 1863 the plaintiff agreed to hire the defendants music hall to give some concerts prior to performance the hall was destroyed by fire and this event, the court held, released the parties from their obligations under the contract. The fact that the parties to a frustrated contract have no further rights or obligations under it could cause hardship.

In January 1963, Edward Condor, the sixteen year old drummer in the Barron Knights pop group, collapsed at a performance and was diagnosed as suffering severe mental strain due to the strenuous nature of the life style associated with his work. The contract the young drummer had signed with Barron Knights Ltd. was for a five year term and required him to perform up to seven nights weekly, sometimes twice nightly. Coupled with the travelling to one night stands this had contributed to his breakdown. The suggestion was made that Condor should only work three or four nights per week but this was rejected as unacceptable by the groups management, and his engagement was terminated. In a claim for damages for breach of contract and wrongful dismissal the High Court concluded that medical condition of the young drummer was such that he was unlikely to be able to continue to perform the obligations required under his contract and accordingly the contract was terminated by virtue of frustration. Justice Thompson said that *"by reason of the impact upon his health and well being of his life, far too strenuous and exhausting for a boy of 16, talented though he was and ambitious though he was, the impact was such in my judgment that had in a business sense made it impossible for him to continue to perform or for the defendants to have him perform the term of the contract as a member of the group."* Certainly the fact that Condor was more than an instrumentalist and an integral part of a highly synchronised comedy routine meant that it would have been very difficult to employ a substitute for those engagements he could not perform.

In the field of concert promotion a good example of a change in circumstances which could frustrate a contract would be withdrawal of the venue due to circumstances beyond the control of the promoter. In *Gamerco SA v ICM/Fair Warning (Agency) Ltd*. 1995 a contract to promote a Guns N' Roses rock concert in a stadium in Madrid was held to be frustrated because the stadium was deemed by Spanish authorities to be unsafe and its use prohibited. The plaintiff promoters were entitled to recover the advance payment of $412,500 from the defendant, the corporate persona of the group Guns N' Roses without any deduction for expenses.

In the analysis of the management contract in Chapter Three there is an example of a force majeure clause designed to provide for the possibility of frustration and the rights of the parties in the event of it occurring.

# Remedies for Breach of Contract

Whenever a breach of contract occurs the innocent party has the option of seeking a remedy from the party in breach. The fundamental quality of contracts is their enforceability and the innocent party has a number of options available to remedy a breach.

# Damages

Damages is the technical term used to describe monetary compensation. Unliquidated damages are those determined by the court exercising its own discretion. The aim is to assess a sum of money that will put the innocent party in the position he would have been in had the contract been performed properly without any breach. The award should not put the innocent party in a better position financially nor should it be intended to punish the contract breaker. Damages may be refused where the court is of the view that they are too speculative.

On this basis the court awarded only nominal damages to the plaintiffs in *Entertainments Ltd. v. Great Yarmouth Borough Council* 1983. The council had repudiated an agreement under which the plaintiffs were to put on summer shows in the town.

The judge, Cantley J took the view that as it had not been established as probable that the shows would have made the plaintiffs a profit, to award anything other than nominal damages would be speculative.

The consequence of a contractual breach can often extend well beyond the immediate obvious losses and lead to a chain of events which become increasingly remote from the immediate breach. The courts take the view that it would be unfair to make a contract breaker responsible for damage caused as a result of circumstances of which he was unaware. Another principle which applies is that the innocent party should take all reasonable steps to mitigate the loss resulting from the breach rather than sitting on the breach. A hotel would be expected to attempt to relet a room that a customer, in breach of contract has fails to use. Damages are not limited to the pure economic cost of the loss of the bargain but may also be recovered for inconvenience, discomfort, distress or anxiety caused by the breach. There are numerous holiday cases where such clauses have been recognised by the courts.

In addition to damages there are also discretionary remedies which may be awarded by the courts. An injunction is a court order to prevent a threatened breach of contract. Such an order would not be made however if it indirectly made the innocent party carry out the terms of a contract involving the provision of services.

An injunction was sought by the manager and publishers of the Troggs pop group in 1967 to prevent them from engaging another manager in breach of contract and from publishing music performed by them other than through themselves. While the High Court agreed that there was a breach of contract, that did not necessarily entitle the management to an injunction. The group and their manager were in a fiduciary relationship and it would be wrong to make the group continue to employ someone in whom they had lost confidence. To prevent them by a court order from going elsewhere was indirectly making them perform a contract involving personal services with their management and the courts will not order an individual to perform obligations under such a contract. The idea of fiduciary duty is explained on pages 71 and 72.

The discretionary remedy of specific performance is designed to require contract breakers perform their obligations under a contract but it will not be ordered in relation to a contract involving personal services.

The reasons for this are that to require performance of such a contract would involve supervision of the contract and the continued good will of the parties. Think of the difficulties attached to ordering an artist to perform a concert particularly in relation to measuring the quality of the performance carried out under duress.

Having explored some of the basic rules of contract law it is now possible to examine three particular music contracts, the management agreement, the record deal and the publishing deal.

The checklists at the beginning of Chapter Three, Four and Five should provide you with some insight into the sort of issues which should be addressed in these types of contracts.

# Management Contract Checklist

Chapter Three contains an analysis of a management agreement term by term. Before a management deal is signed the parties to it should be aware of the following:

* What is the term of the contract and how long can it be extended?

* Does the contract expire at the end of the initial term if the manager fails to trigger an extension?

* Does the contract provide for a trial or probationary period of six months or so to enable the parties to establish their credentials and commitment?

* If the artist is a band

    * who are the key members?

    * how are earnings divided?

    * what are the consequences of a breach of contract by one member of the band?

    * what is the position in the event of a leaving member?

* What are the duties of the manager under the contract?

* Is the management's role restricted to music, or management, or does it relate to the entertainment industry generally?

* In what circumstances can the contract be terminated or suspended by the management?

* What is the earnings capacity of the management following termination of the contract?

* Who is responsible for dealing with finance for example:

    * who collects the earnings and how are they calculated?

    * who is responsible for expenses and how are they calculated?

    * what is the management's commission and how is it calculated?

    * what are the accounting provisions?

# Chapter Three
## Management Agreements

Management contracts or management agreements as they are usually called set out the relationship between a *management organisation,* which could be an individual a partnership or a company and the *artist,* which could be an individual or a group of individuals, in other words a band. There is nothing significant in calling the relationship an agreement rather than a contract, for like a tenancy agreement with a landlord, or a holiday agreement with a tour operator, the relationship between a manager and an artist is contractual in nature.

The commencement of any contract in the music business will provide for the date and the names and addresses of the parties to the agreement. If the manager is a company it must have a registered address and if the artist is a band then the names and addresses of all the members must be included. You should appreciate from the outset that the fact that the artist is composed of a number of members does not mean that they necessarily have the same status under the contract, and the same entitlement to remuneration. Obviously in most bands there are significant members who can be given *key member status*, and this means that they are more likely to remain tied to the management in the event that the band splits up.

An important legal expression to be aware of where a number of band members sign a management or recording contract is the use of the phrase *"joint and several"*. It often appears in the first clause of a contract and is usually overlooked. It refers to the fact that the members of the band are *'jointly'* liable under the contract but more significantly if their liability is *'several'* they can also be sued individually. This could mean that potentially one member of a band could be made liable for the breaches of another. This is the usual routine in a partnership contract where the individual partners are liable jointly and severally for broken contracts with other parties. The potential risks of liability for the breach of contract by another member should be explained to the individual contracting parties.

Earlier in Chapter One I referred to the recent High Court decision in *Martin-Smith v Williams* 1998 where the judge confirmed that the manager of an artist will normally owe him a fiduciary duty of good faith. If the artist is a band it is important to appreciate that this duty is owed not only to the band as a whole but also to the individual members within it. One assertion put forward by lawyers for Robbie Williams was that the manager was in breach of what is called the double employment rule in that he had put the interests of the rest of the band before those of Robbie Williams. While the court rejected this assertion on the facts before them, I would still maintain that it is a legal principle which all band managers should be aware of. The words of Lord Justice Millett from the Court of Appeal decision in *Bristol & West Building Society v Matthew* 1996 are particularly relevant. He said that *"Even if a fiduciary (a manager) is properly acting for two principals (band members) with potentially conflicting interests he must act in good faith in the interests of each and must not act with the intention of furthering the interests of one principal to the prejudice of those of the other.... He must not allow the performance of his obligations to one principal to be influenced by the relationship with the other. He must serve each as faithfully and legally as if he were his only principal. Conduct which is in breach of duty need not be dishonest but it must be intentional. An unconscious omission which happens to benefit one principal at the expense of the other does not constitute a breach of fiduciary duty, though it may constitute a breach of the duty of skill and care."*

# Definitions and Interpretations

All standard form contracts in the music business will contain language and terminology where understanding depends upon precise interpretation. For this reason all such contracts will contain a Definitions and Interpretations clause usually as the initial term of the contract. Here words and phrases found in the contract are given precise definitions. It is tempting to ignore such a term when analysing a contract and to start with the substance of the agreement. Certainly the definition term needs to be referred to when interpreting the substance of the agreement but in my view contracting parties should be aware of some of the standard definitions employed in the music contracts, for the rights and obligations of the parties to the contract often turn on such definitions. When we analyse the substance of the contract we will refer to definitions but I thought at this stage it would be useful to comment on some of the more controversial definitions contained in a model contract.

1   *'Entertainment Industry' means any form of entertainment or leisure activity now known or existing during the Term including:*

   *motion picture film television radio broadcasting diffusion video and audio-visual recording;*

   *live stage variety cabaret club entertainment live performance vaudeville review personal appearance and associated or similar activities literature art music drama choreography and advertising sponsorship or merchandising.*

If the contract provides that management is to extend to the participation of the artist in the *"entertainment industry"* then the definition contained in the model term will usually apply. This is entirely suitable if the artist wishes the management company to control all aspects of his career but would not be suitable in all cases. An established artist may wish to retain exclusive control over one or more areas such as publishing, personal appearances or film work and engage more specialist management for these purposes. In such circumstances it would be advisable to ensure that the definition suits the needs and requirements of the artist.

> 2 *'Artist's Advances' means all loans and other advances made to the Artist by the Manager (or by an Associate of the Manager) together with any other expenditure of the Manager including without limitation agency fees and commissions interest expenses relating to travelling, accommodation, transport, purchase or hire of equipment and all sums expenses and fees relating to engagement of tour managers, road managers, personal assistants, publicity consultants and all expenditure on advertising and publicity of all descriptions public relations entertaining legal advice and/or services and accountancy services.*

Artist advances are of course recoverable from the artist's earnings and in the model term we have a very wide definition of the range of payments which could be included within that definition. Certainly it seems reasonable that all loans and cash payments by the management to the artist are recoverable as advances. There could be some concern however by the artist that the remaining expenditure envisaged is regarded as an advance. Artists advances are not classified as a debt. They are recoverable from royalties but there is no legal requirement to repay them if there turns out to be insufficient income. Advances represent the investment of the Management in the Artist.

Obviously it is the artist who must 'foot the bill' for the expenditure identified but it is arguable as to whether it should be regarded as an advance. If it is to be included as an advance it would still be possible to place a limit on sums expended, for instance in relation to public relations entertaining and legal advice.

> 3 *'Expenses' means all expenditure of the Manager directly or indirectly incurred in connection with the Management Services including in particular but not by way of limitation transportation, travel, accommodation, entertaining, telephone, office expenses and legal and accountancy fees.*

This model term identifies the range of direct and indirect expenses which may be incurred in providing the artist with management services and we will see that the contract will purport to deduct these expenses from the artist's income. An artist could be advised that it is excessive for a management company to include the indirect expenditure of office overheads as expenses given that it is by incurring such overheads that the management company is enabled to earn its commission. It should be possible to distinguish between the expense of an overnight stay in an hotel to visit the artist on tour and the cost of phone calls. The former as direct expenditure should be recoverable while the latter an indirect expenditure could be excluded. The treatment of expenses will depend very much on whether the manager's commission is levied on the artist's gross or net earnings. As far as legal expenses are concerned the artist should be made aware as to whether the legal costs of setting up the management agreement are included as expenses. Later we shall discover the importance of the artist seeking legal advice on the form of the management agreement and there should be agreement as to who bears the cost of such advice.

> 4 *'Gross Income' means 100% of all sums arising pursuant to any Engagement Agreement at source directly or indirectly payable credited or receivable by or on behalf of the Artist the Manager or any Associate or agent or representative associated of the artist or any company or joint venture with which the artist is associated in the Territory in respect of the Services*

> *including the arm's length cash value of any Goods or any 'in kind' arrangement directly or indirectly payable credited receivable to made available to or on behalf of the Artist or any Associate or agent or representative of the Artist.*

Determining the gross income of the artist may be crucial in deciding the commission payable to the management company for its services. The parties should be clear as to what constitutes gross income and appreciate that the model term gives the expression a very wide definition. Obviously the more inflated the gross income, the larger the chunk of commission payable to a management company receiving commission as a percentage of gross earnings. Gross income could be limited to the amount of money actually received by the artist and exclude any sums payable to associates, agents or representatives of any company. It may be that an artist would wish to exclude from gross income the value from any 'in kind' goods given to the artist such as jewellery. It should be stressed that payments from a record company as 'tour support' would also fall within this definition of gross income unless excluded.

> 5  *'Event of Force Majeure' means act of God including but not limited to fire flood earthquake windstorm or other natural disaster; act of any sovereign including but not limited to war invasion act of foreign enemies hostilities whether war be declared or not civil war rebellion revolution insurrection military or usurped power or confiscation nationalisation requisition destruction or damage to property by or under the order of government or public or local authority or imposition of government sanction embargo or similar action law judgement order decree embargo blockage or labour dispute including but not limited to strike lock out or boycott; interruption or failure of utility service including but not limited to electric power gas water or telephone service; failure of the transportation of any personnel equipment machinery supply or*

*material required by the Manager; breach of contract by any essential person; any other matter or cause beyond the control of the Manager.*

*Force majeure* is considered in Chapter Two and this is a standard form definition which appears in all music contracts to identify the circumstances which could frustrate the contract. The express term dealing with frustration rarely seeks to terminate the contract but rather provides for its suspension during the period of frustration. This means effectively that the management are prevented from making use of the artist's services during the period of frustration.

Having considered some of the main definitions in the contract it is now possible to examine the express contractual terms.

Quite often the contract will list the express terms under a series of headings such as:

1. *Management Appointment;*

2. *Options;*

3. *Managers Undertakings;*

4. *Artist Undertakings;*

5. *Group Provisions;*

6. *Suspension;*

7. *Termination.*

# 1. Appointment

1.1 *In consideration of the undertakings of the Manager contained in this Agreement the Artist irrevocably appoints the Manager as the Artist's sole and exclusive agent during the Term to negotiate conclude and execute Engagement Agreements on*

> *behalf of the Artist in respect of the Services*
> *throughout the Territory whether during or after the*
> *Term for the purpose of which the Artist irrevocably*
> *appoints the Manager as the Artist's true and lawful*
> *attorney throughout the Territory during the Term*
> *and undertakes to ratify and confirm whatever the*
> *Manager shall do or purport to do pursuant to such*
> *power of attorney.*

Here we have a standard model term which seeks to attain the fundamental object of a management contract - the appointment of the manager. The aim is to confer extensive authority on the manager as agent to have the exclusive rights to negotiate and enter into engagement contracts on behalf of the artist throughout the world. By giving the manager power of attorney the artist is conferring official power on the manager to act on his behalf in legal matters. Clearly the term as drafted will not suit all artists, for instance

* management could be restricted to a geographical area e.g. the world excluding North America;

* contractual power could be limited to negotiating contracts rather than concluding them;

* it may not be in the best interest of the artist to confer power of attorney.

> *1.2    The Artist irrevocably grants to the Manager the*
> *sole and exclusive right and authority on behalf of*
> *the Artist to collect and receive all Gross Income*
> *arising out of Engagement Agreements during the*
> *Term and after the expiry of the Term to the extent*
> *such Gross Income arises out of Engagement*
> *Agreements negotiated by the Manager during the*
> *Term.*

The manager's right to have sole and exclusive authority over the collection of gross income during the term of the contract is a fundamental feature of the contract and is unassailable. In practice of course established managers do not handle money and engage qualified accountants to collect income and distribute commision.

This traditional model term seeks to confer control over gross income to the manager even after the conclusion of the managerial contract in relation to those engagement contracts (record deals etc.) entered into during the term of the management contract. The right to commission in such circumstances has been the subject of litigation and contemporary case-law is considered in Chapter Two.

The contract could of course make the rights to such payment conditional upon there being no breach of contract by the management which would have prematurely led to a contractual termination. For a serious breach of contract the injured party has the option of terminating the contract. It is called accepting a repudiatory breach of contract.

> *1.3 The Artist agrees that the Artist shall not negotiate Engagement Agreements but shall refer all interests or enquiries to the Manager.*
>
> *1.4 The Artist undertakes forthwith to account to the Manager for all sums received or receivable by the Artist in connection with Engagement Agreements.*
>
> *1.5 The Manager shall have the right on behalf of the Artist to do any acts and take any steps including without limitation the commencement of legal proceedings in the name of the Artist in order to enforce the provisions of any Engagement Agreement or to collect any sums owing or otherwise to protect the rights granted to the Manager under this Agreement.*

*1.6    The Artist undertakes to do any and all acts and execute any and all documents that may be required by the Manager from time to time in connection with the rights granted to the Manager under this agreement.*

*1.7    Nothing in this Agreement shall expressly or impliedly impose any obligation on the Manager to act as an 'employment agency' or be concerned in the 'employment business' as those terms are defined in the Employment Agencies Act 1973 Section 13 and the Artist acknowledges that the Manager is not the holder of a licence under that Act.*

Contractual terms which restrict the authority of the artist to negotiate engagement contracts, to account to the manager for any sum of money received and to cooperate with management by given written assent to documentation, are all necessary to ensure the operation of the management contract. While it seems reasonable that the management should have authority to take legal steps to enforce engagement agreements the artist may wish to place a limit on the expenditure which could be incurred for this purpose.

There is no requirement under this type of contract to obtain an employment agency licence.

*1.8    The Manager shall throughout the Territory during the Term have the sole and exclusive right to authorise and arrange publication of any articles by or concerning the Artist and any biography or autobiography of the Artist in any newspapers magazines books and other printed material including expressly audio and audio-visual tapes and to authorise others to use and exploit the name likeness and biography of the Artist by any means in all media in connection with the endorsement promotion advertising and publicity of any and all products and services*

This term may be perfectly acceptable if the purpose of the contract is to enable the management to have sole exclusive rights to promote the artist through any means suitable. On the other hand a well established artist may only wish to co-operate with interviews and product endorsements and sponsorship following consultation with the management and indeed retain the final say in relation to such matters.

## 2. Options

2.1   *In consideration of the undertakings of the Manager contained in this Agreement the Artist irrevocably grants to the Manager the following options (the 'Options') to extend the appointment of the Manager exercisable by notice in writing at any time before the expiry of each relevant period.*

*the sole and exclusive option to extend the Initial Period by the First Option Period (the 'First' Option)*

*the sole and exclusive option to extend the First Option Period by the Second Option Period (the 'Second' Option)*

*The Second Option may only be exercised if the First Option has been exercised.*

2.2   *If the Manager fails to exercise any of the Options on or before the due date this Agreement shall remain in full force and effect until the Manager shall have received notice in writing signed by all of the Members of the Artist requiring the Manager to exercise the Option and following receipt of such notice the Manager shall have [45] days in which to do so.*

The options term in a management contract is purely for the benefit of the manager and there is no corresponding clause conferring option rights on the Artist. The purpose of the option clause is to authorise the management to unilaterally extend the period of the contract by a further period called the first option period. There is no requirement to obtain the agreement of the artist to such an extension but presumably such agreement will be sought by the management. Depending on the status of the artist the option clause could provide that an advance should be paid to the artist each time the management exercises its option to extend the period of the contract.

On the expiration of the first option period there is a further right for the manager to extend the term of the contract by a second option period. The validity of lengthy contracts was considered in Chapter One but it does seem reasonable that the artist should be made aware from the outset the potential period of time he could be contracted to the management, should the first and second option periods be taken up. Given the nature of the music business and the limited potential of an artist to be successful it does seem reasonable that if a management company has contributed to the success of an artist then it should have the capacity in the contract to obtain some benefit from that success beyond the initial period of the contract. On this basis option periods can be justified, I do however find clause 2.2 a startling proposition.

The clause provides that if the management fails to exercise an option to renew the contract on the due date then this is not fatal to the contract for it will continue automatically until the artist serves notice on the management requiring them to exercise the option to renew. If such a notice is served on the management even then the management has a further period to exercise the renewal option and failure to do so will terminate the contract. I am at a loss to determine how long the contract will continue automatically (presumably for a reasonable length of time) if the artist fails to serve notice on the management.

An assertion put forward in *Martin-Smith v Williams* 1998 was that following the termination of the first option period there was an oral agreement between the Manager and Take That to the effect that the management agreement should extend for an indefinite duration subject to termination by any party on six months notice. A reduction in Mr Martin-Smith's commission from 25% to 20% was also agreed in the presence of lawyers representing the manager and the band. There was no dispute by Robbie Williams that this agreement took place but whether it was made subject to contract. The judge held that there was no evidence that the agreement was subject to contract and that the oral agreement to extend the contractual term indefinitely subject to notice was legally binding.

## 3.  Manager's Undertakings

> *Subject to the performance and observance by the Artist of all of the Artists warranties and obligations and undertakings this Agreement the Manager undertakes with the Artist:*

> *3.1  To render the Management Services for the benefit of the Artist and to use all reasonable endeavours to conclude Engagement Agreements on behalf of the Artist for the Services throughout the Term and to maximise receipts from them.*

> *3.2  To act as reasonable time and places during normal business hours as the Artist's manager and adviser in connection with the Services.*

> *3.3  To appoint any agent licensed under the Employment Agencies Act 1973 that is deemed necessary by the Manager for the purposes of*

> *furthering the Artist's career and to pay all*
> *commissions and fees of such agent as expenses.*

It is in this term that the contract spells out the obligations of the manager, in other words, what he promises to do on behalf of the artist under the contract. There is a clear indication in the first paragraphs that the undertakings included are subject to the artist fulfilling his side of the bargain so that if the artist is in breach of contract the management is no longer obliged to fulfil its obligations. Under 3.1 the requirement to render management services and conclude engagement agreements is subject to using *reasonable endeavours*. There could also be a requirement to use *best endeavours* to promote the career of the artist, and such an aim could be encouraged by paying the artist an advance on his signature.

In the management agreement entered into by Take That and Mr Martin-Smith there was an important clause which provided that *"you will use all reasonable endeavours to enhance and develop our career in the area of activity referred to in clause 1 and will generally render all services customarily rendered by a manager in the entertainment industry."*

The requirement under 3.2 to act at reasonable times and places during normal business hours might not be acceptable to an artist who needs to have full-time world-wide access to their management. The right to appoint agents on behalf of the artist could also be subject to consultation or approval. It does seem that those few qualified obligations of the management could, depending on status of the artist, be extended to include promoting the artist and exploiting his commercial opportunity subject to the artist retaining control over his career.

## 4.   Artist's Undertakings

> *As a material inducement towards the Manager to*
> *enter into this Agreement the Artist warrants*
> *undertakes and agrees with the Manager that:*

4.1    *The Artist has attained the age of 18 years*

4.2    *The Artist is free to enter into this Agreement and grant to the Manager the rights granted in it and is not under any disability restriction or prohibition which might prevent the Artist from performing or observing any of the Artist's obligations under this Agreement*

4.3    *The Artist has not entered into and shall not enter into any arrangement which might conflict with this Agreement*

4.4    *The Artist shall not without the prior written consent of the Manager incur any expenditure or costs on behalf of the Manager*

4.5    *The Artist is and shall become and shall remain throughout the Term a member in good standing of all unions and guilds the membership of which may be lawfully required for the performance of the Services.*

The artist will be required to agree to numerous undertakings under the contract and this term should give you some idea as to their nature and extent. Certainly there is an obvious disparity between the extent of the artists undertakings and the management undertakings under the contract. Most of the obligations are quite strict and unlike the management undertakings are not qualified by the expression *"using reasonable endeavours"*. In 4.1 to 4.5 the artist confirms that he has capacity to enter into the contract as a free agent, over 18, who is unionised where necessary.

4.6    *The Artist shall not without the consent in writing of the Manager disclose reveal or make public information of any nature in connection with the business of the Manager or the terms of this*

> *Agreement all of which shall be treated by the Artist on a strictly confidential basis*

An express confidentiality clause is contained in 4.6. Such clauses are now common place in contracts of employment and are recognised as perfectly acceptable in protecting the interests of the manager. There could however be some justification in including a similar term in the management undertakings under which the management agrees to respect the confidentiality of the artist.

> *4.7    The Artist shall not issue any publicity relating to the Services or participate in any interview or other publicity without the prior written consent of the Manager*

It may be acceptable to a new artist particularly in a manufactured band to agree that the management should control all publicity in relation to the artist and that is the essence of 4.7. On the other hand it may be unacceptable to the artist to have to obtain the written consent of the management before participating in an interview.

> *4.8    The Artist shall not any time during the Term render Services pursuant to any Engagement Agreement which has been negotiated by the Manager*

While the aim of 4.8 is to limit the artist exclusively to carrying out engagements negotiated by the management it could be the case that there are previous contractual commitments which must be honoured and the clause could be amended to accommodate them.

> *4.9    The Artist shall render all Services require pursuant to Engagement Agreements to the best of the Artist's skill and ability in a professional punctual and workmanlike manner in willing co-operation with others*

*4.10   The Artist shall at all times pay due and proper attention to the personal appearance and make up of the Artist*

*4.11   The Artist shall take all practical steps to preserve and maintain the health of the Artist at all times throughout the Term and to comply with the requirements of the insurer's of the Manager in order to enable the manager to effect and maintain insurance against loss arising from the Artist's inability to perform the Services on normal terms and conditions at basic premium rates*

*4.12   The Artist shall not commit any act which might prejudice or damage the reputation of the Manager or might inhibit restrict or interfere with the successful exploitation of the Services*

*4.13   The Artist shall disclose to the Manager all proper agreements and arrangements relating to the Artist's Services*

*4.14   The Artist shall not at any time during the Term take part in any dangerous pursuits or voluntarily take any risks which might at any time interfere with the ability of the Artist to perform the Artist's obligations and Services under this Agreement*

In clauses 4.9 to 4.14 the management extracts undertakings from the artist in relation to professionalism and maintaining health to ensure the proper performance of engagement contracts. Such clauses seem perfectly acceptable given that it is in the best interest of the artist to ensure he has the capacity to carry out engagement contracts to the best of his ability.

*4.15   The Artist shall undertake such training and instruction as the Manager may consider reasonable and do all reasonable acts or things that*

> *the Manager may from time to time advise for the fulfilment of any Engagement Agreement*

The requirement under 4.15 to participate in training and instruction may be necessary for a manufactured artist consisting of talented individuals brought together to form a coherent band. It is unlikely however that an established artist would find such a clause acceptable as an absolute obligation, and may require some modification to qualify it.

> *4.16    The Artist shall comply with all rules regulations and agreements relating to safety fire prevention or general administration that may be in force at any place where the Artist may be required to render Serves under this Agreement*

> *4.17    The Artist undertakes to refer to the Manager all enquiries which the Artist may receive during the Term relating to the proposed engagement of the Artist as a performer*

> *4.18    The Artist undertakes not without the consent of the Manager to change to Professional Name in whole or part or to perform under any other name*

Clauses 4.16 and 4.17 are straightforward and necessary while 4.18 seeks to preserve the goodwill that attaches to the name of the artist.

> *4.19    The Artist shall at all times throughout the Term keep the Manager informed of the Artist's whereabouts and telephone number*

> *4.20    The manager has advised the Artist of the Artist's rights to seek legal advice on the consents of this Agreement and has given the Artist every opportunity to take such advice and the Artist acknowledges that the Artist has to take such advice*

*from a solicitor experienced in Agreements of this nature and the Artist has read and fully understood all of the provisions of this Agreement*

There is case law considered in Chapter One which demonstrates the need for 4.20 to enable the contract to be enforced. It is a crucial part of the contract which must be included to ensure that the agreement is legally binding

4.21 *The Artist undertakes to indemnify the Manager and keep the Manager at all times fully indemnified from and against all actions proceedings claims demands costs (including without prejudice to the generality of this provision legal costs of the Manager on a solicitor and own client basis) awards and damages however arising directly or indirectly as a result of any breach or non-performance by the Artist of any of the Artist's undertakings warranties or obligations under this Agreement*

Under 4.21 the artist agrees that in the event of a breach of contract he will indemnify the manager against the payment of any legal costs that he may incur.

## 5. Group Provisions

In the event that the Artist comprises more than one Member the terms and provisions of this clause shall apply. The relevant clause in the management agreement entered into between 'Take That and Mr Martin-Smith is

5.1 *Each of us acknowledge that in this Agreement the singular shall include the plural and vice-versa and that this Agreement applies to us both in our capacity as a member of a group and in respect of all other activities of each of us in the entertainment industry and the product of such activities whether together, as an individual or as a member of any*

> *other    group    or    otherwise    howsoever.    We*
> *acknowledge that each of the terms and conditions*
> *of the Agreement shall apply to each of us jointly*
> *and severally.*

This clause is highly significant if the artist is composed of a band. The meaning of joint and several liability is discussed at the beginning of the Chapter and it means of course that each member of the band is potentially liable jointly and individually in the event of a breach of the management contract. The clause does provide however that the manager manages each member of the band individually as well as the band as a whole. This is an important point if there is a relationship breakdown within the band. As Mr Martin-Smith discovered with 'Take That' he should not take sides in the event of acrimony within the band.

> 5.2    *In the event of any breach of the Artist obligation*
> *and warranties in the Agreement by any Member of*
> *Members the Manager shall have a right to treat*
> *such breaches as a breach or repudiation by all*
> *Members and each Member shall be jointly and*
> *severally liable.*

5.2 makes it clear that an individual band member could be made individually liable for a breach by another member in the same way that in a partnership contract the individual partners are potentially liable for each other's actions. This is of course a startling proposition, particularly when you consider that a management contract unlike a partnership contract is not one of utmost good faith. A conscientious band member could under 5.2 be made liable for the unprofessional conduct of another over whom he has no control.

> 5.3    *Each Member undertakes that no change of*
> *membership of the Artist shall occur without the*
> *prior written consent of the Manager and in the*
> *event that any Member proposes to leave the Artist*

> *that Member shall forthwith give the Manager notice in writing of the proposal ('Leaving Notice').*

> 5.4   *Each Member acknowledges that such Member shall relinquish all rights in and to the Professional Name of the Artist on receipt by the Manager of a Leaving Notice from that Member but that the other provisions of this Agreement shall remain in full force and effect in respect of the Artist's future activities and any new professional name of the Artist.*

> 5.5   *All sums payable to the Artist by the Manager pursuant to this Agreement shall be divided between the Members in the following percentages:....*

If a band member leaves the band without securing the approval of the management then the Artist is in breach of contract. Having said that it would not be advisable to attempt to restrain an unhappy band member from leaving given the acrimony that this would cause. Most certainly the courts would not order the performance of a contract involving the provision of services so that if faced with a leaving notice the most prudent course would be to secure a satisfactory replacement as quickly and sensitively as possible.

In *Martin-Smith v Williams* 1998 one of the allegations made by lawyers on behalf of Robbie Williams was that his manager, Mr Martin-Smith was in breach of the management contract, in particular his fiduciary duty to act in the best interests of Robbie Williams to promote his career within the entertainment field. This duty was broken it was alleged by the manager advising the rest of the band 'Take That' that they should counsel Robbie Williams to leave the band if he could not commit himself to it. William's lawyers pleaded that in relation to his dealings with their client the manager necessarily and unavoidably placed himself in conflict with their client's interests and consequently put him in breach of duty. Such breach went to the heart of the relationship and was necessarily repudiatory in nature. This meant they agreed that Williams could accept the serious breach of contract and treat the management contract as terminated.

The judge accepted that if this conduct had occurred it would indeed constitute a breach of fiduciary duty by the manager. His view of the evidence was however that rather than counselling Mr Williams to leave, the manager had in fact put forward a number of options and this itself did not put him in breach of his fiduciary duty. Justice Ferris said that *"I cannot see how the advice which I have found Mr Martin-Smith to have given to Gary Barlow and Jason Orange can be said to have affected the performance of his duties to Robbie Williams. If the group was to continue as before it was as important to Robbie Williams as the other members of the group that the forthcoming tours should be successful. Apart from the damage to the reputation of the group there would be serious adverse financial consequences to all the members of the group if for any reason the group failed to fulfil its commitments Mr Martin-Smith clearly believed that the avoidance of these consequences required that matters were resolved immediately, either on the basis of a long term commitment of the group to each other or on the basis of an immediate break. I am sure that if the occasion had arisen Mr Martin-Smith would have given the same advice to all members of the group both collectively and individually."* In deciding that the manager was not in breach of contract as a consequence Robbie Williams was not entitled to treat the contract as terminated and remained bound by its terms including the requirement to give six months notice to terminate the contract.

Even if it is a key member of the band who is leaving. 5.4 makes it clear that he has no claim on the band name. While the contract could provide that the band members share income equally, this is not necessarily always the case and it could be that the percentage earnings will vary according to the contributions made by the individual band members.

# 6.  Artists Obligations

*Without the prior written consent of the Manager the Artist undertakes not to:*

6.1   *Render any Services (whether paid or unpaid) to any third party*

6.2   *Vary any term or condition of any Engagement Agreement whether orally or in writing or by a course of conduct*

6.3   *Employ or engage any person in respect of the Artist's career in the Entertainment Industry.*

Clause 6 of the contract is an express term imposing obligations on the Artist to:

*perform exclusively on engagement contracts negotiated by the management;*

*comply strictly with any engagement agreement and make no attempt to vary the terms;*

*refrain from employing any individual in connection with his career.*

The clause restricts the unauthorised unpaid activities of the artist for which of course no management commission would be payable. To prevent the Artist from unilaterally changing engagement agreements seems reasonable but many artists will want to engage their own advisors and to such artists 6.3 might be unacceptable.

# 7.  Application of Gross Income

7.1   *The Manager shall have the right to deduct and retain from Gross Income from the manager's own use and benefit absolutely the following items in the following order*

*the Commission*

*the Expenses*

*the Artist's Advances*

*interest on the amount (if any) unrecovered of the Expenses and the Artist's Advances at the rate 2½% above the base rate from time to time of the (name of bank)*

*such reasonable reserve against future Expenses and Artist's Advances as the Manager in its entire discretion deems appropriate.*

7.2    *Subject to and conditional upon the full and timely performance and observance by the Artist of the obligations and warranties of the Artist under this Agreement the balance of Gross Income remaining after the deduction of the items listed clauses above shall be remitted to the Artist in accordance with the provisions of the clause.*

This is the clause which determines how the income of the Artist is shared and more than any other term should be explained in detail to the artist. Gross income, advances and expenses, are of course defined in the definition clause of the contract and the parties should be clear as to their meaning to appreciate the division of income under clause 7.

Commission is usually payable on gross income earned during the term and from deals negotiated during the term. The issue in *Martin-Smith v Williams* 1998 was whether commission was payable on Robbie Williams earnings which he alleged were made after he had terminated the management agreement in response to the manager's breach of fiduciary duty.

The most striking feature of the clause is that it provides that the commission of the management (15% or 20%) is payable out of gross income. The gross income of an artist represents his turnover which could amount to a high figure so providing a healthy commission for the management. Once the expenses, advances and reserves have been deducted, however, to produce a net income, the remaining sum could represent a small return for the artist. This net amount must then be divided in a band to provide each member with their appropriate percentage of income. Managers are of course reluctant to earn commission based on net income.

The amount of the commission will depend entirely on the nature of the relationship between the manager and the artist. Obviously in cases where the manager has promoted the career of an artist from relative obscurity to established status the percentage may be higher. If the manager has created the artist, invested capital, and secured major publishing and recording deals he will expect quite a high return in the event of success. Mr Martin-Smith was entitled to 25% of the gross receipts of 'Take That' in respect of recording or publishing contracts entered into or *"substantially negotiated"* during the term of the Management Agreement.

## 8. Accounting

8.1 *The Manager shall render to the Artist within [90] days after 30 June and 31 December in each year any positive statement of account relating to the preceding 6 month period indicating all sums due to the Artist in accordance with the provisions of this Agreement and accompanied by the payment of the amount indicated by such statements to be owing.*

8.2   *The first of the accounting statements shall be rendered at the end of the first full period immediately following the date of this Agreement and shall be deemed to be binding on the parties to this Agreement unless the Artist shall within [90] days from receipt of any statement request that it be certified by the auditors of the Manager. Such certification shall be at the cost and expense of the Artist and shall be final and binding on the parties to this Agreement.*

The accounting provisions of the contract provide for six monthly accounts to be produced and submitted to the Artist for approval. The statements must indicate the amount payable to the artist and also include the payment. Under clause 8.2 there is machinery to trigger an audit of the accounts but this would be at the expense of the artist.

## 9.   Manager's Activities

*The Manager shall have the right without being in breach of any fiduciary obligations or duties to the Artist at any time during the Term whether alone or in conjunction with others:*

*to act as agent or manager for any other artist or group*

*to acquire literary dramatic or musical rights from the Artist*

*to grant on behalf of the Artist all consents required pursuant to the Copyright, Designs and Patents Act 1988 Part II in connection with the performances of the Artists pursuant to the Engagement Agreements*

A fiduciary duty arises when a person is acting in a position of trust in relation to another. A company director owes a fiduciary duty towards the company. This term acknowledges the fiduciary duty owed by a manager to the artist but states that the position of trust is not broken if the manager acts for another artist, acquires rights from the artist, acts as a promoter of the artist or enters into a recording or publishing contract with artist. Any of those activities could of course be excluded from the contract. With a band of course the fiduciary duty extends to each individual member.

In Chapter One we considered the case of *Clifford Davis v WEA Records* 1975 where there was held to be a conflict of interest when a manager also acted as the publishing company of the artist. The dilemma of this type of scenario is that the manager on behalf of the artist may negotiate a publishing deal with himself in the form of another organisation.

As far as acting for the other artists is concerned it could be that a band with a high status may wish to restrict the manager from engaging other competing bands in the same field under management agreements.

## 10. Suspension

*The Manager shall be entitled by notice to the Artist to suspend the Term and the engagement of the Services if:*

*10.1  the Artist refuses or fails to perform any of the Services or refuse or fails to perform or observe or is otherwise in breach of any of the obligations undertakings or warranties on the part of the Artist contained in this Agreement.*

*10.2  the Artist shall have failed to submit to any medical examination required by the Manager or any insurance company or shall have made any untrue statements or inaccurate replies on any proposals* for insurance of the Manager shall have been able to obtain insurance in respect of the Artist on normal terms and conditions at normal premiums.

10.3 the Artist shall have been prevented from performing the Services or shall be in the opinion of the Manager incapable of performing the Services whether as a result or injury illness mental or physical disability or otherwise for a period of (number) consecutive [days of weeks] after the date when the Services were required.

10.4 the appearance personality or voice of the Artist shall for whatever reason have materially deteriorated in the opinion of the Manager and such material deterioration shall continue for a period of (number) consecutive [days or weeks] after the date when the Services were required or

10.5 and Event of Force Majeure shall prevent the Manager from making use of the Services.

The purpose of this clause is to prolong the term of the contract in the event that the Artist cannot for any period perform his obligations under it. In the event of a wilful refusal to perform, or other breach of contract by the artist, the management can serve notice on the artist that the contract is suspended during the period of the breach. The circumstances that could trigger a suspension also include the inability to perform through illness or injury or psychological problems and events of force majeure (see Chapter One).

## 11. Termination

11.1 The Manager shall have the right to terminate this Agreement or accept the repudiation by the Artist of this Agreement at any time when the Manager is entitled to serve notice of suspension pursuant to the

*provisions of clause 10.1 or 10.2 or at any time
following the expire of [14] days after the Manager
shall have given notice of suspension pursuant to
any of clauses 10.3 to 10.5 inclusive.*

Clause 11.1 provides that the right to suspend the agreement
under clause 10, for example for breach of contract, also
confers the right on the management to terminate the agreement.
Additionally if a notice of suspension has been served the
management could, after a period, terminate the contract. The
expression *"accept a repudiation"* means that the innocent party
has the option of terminating the contract in response to the
others serious or repudiatory breach.

*The following provisions shall apply on or after notice of
termination by the Manager:*

*11.2   the Artist shall continue to apply to comply with all
of the obligations on the part of the Artist under this
Agreement which are not affected by termination.*

*11.3   the Manager shall remain entitled to all rights
granted or assigned to the Manager under this
Agreement and all other rights relating to the
Services and the entire product of the Services.*

*11.4   the Artist shall be entitled only to such
remuneration as shall have accrued due and
become payable at the date of termination or the
date suspension if earlier.*

*11.5   Any claim which either party may have against the
other in respect of any breach or non-performance
or repudiation of any of the provisions of this
Agreement which shall have occurred prior to such
termination or suspension shall not be affected or
prejudiced and all rights of suspension or
termination under this Agreement are in addition to*

> *and separate from any other rights of the Manager
> at law.*

Clause 11 attempts to set out the legal position in the event that
a notice of termination is served by the management. Its main
purpose is to ensure that the management rights in relation to
assignment of copyright and remuneration on products produced
secured during the term of the contract are secured. There is an
express statement that legal claims which have arisen prior to
notice of termination are unaffected by the notice and such
claims can be pursued despite the agreement coming to an end.

## 12. No Liability

The Manager shall not be liable to the Artist under any
circumstances whatever in respect of any claim for loss of
opportunity on the part of the Artist to enhance the Artist's
reputation.

## 13. Insurance

> *The Manager may secure in its own name or otherwise
> and at its own cost and expense life insurance accident
> insurance or health insurance and any other insurance
> required by the Manager in respect of the Artists.*

Clause 13 reflects the fact that the artist may be a major asset of
the management company's business and consequently it would
be prudent to take out life/accidental/health insurance in respect
of the artist. It is a basic principle of insurance law that the
manager has an insurable interest in the life of the artist and
vice-versa. Suprisingly it seems that most managers do not
insure their artists and yet most record companies do.

## 14. Severability

*If any provision of this Agreement shall be prohibited by or adjudged by a court to be unlawful void or unenforceable such provision shall to the extent required be served from this Agreement and rendered ineffective as far as possible without modifying the remaining provisions of this Agreement and shall not in any way affect any other circumstances or the validity or enforcement of this Agreement.*

The object of clause 14 is to ensure that if part of the contract turns out to be void (of no legal effect) or unenforceable (not actionable before a court) this will have no impact on the rest of the contract which will remain valid and enforceable.

## 15. Agreement Final and Complete

*This agreement contains the full and completed understanding between the parties and supersedes all pervious arrangements and understandings whether written or oral appertaining to the subject matter of this Agreement and may not be varied except by an instrument in writing signed by all of the parties to this Agreement.*

Clause 15 purports to provide that the contract represents the *"deal"* between the parties and overrides any other written or oral agreement. In addition the parties accept that no oral promises were made in respect of the contract which could constitute representations and be regarded as actionable mirepresentations if proved to be false.

## 16. Waiver

*No failure or delay on the part of any of the parties to this Agreement relating to the exercise of any right power privilege or remedy provided under this Agreement shall operate as a waiver of such right power privilege or remedy or as a waiver of any preceding or succeeding breach by the other party to this Agreement nor shall any single or partial exercise of any right power privilege or remedy preclude any other or further exercise of such or any other right power privilege or remedy provided in this Agreement all of which are several and cumulative and are not exclusive of each other or of any other rights or remedies otherwise available to a party or law or in equity.*

Clause 16 discounts the possibility of an implied waiver in relation to a breach of contract caused by delay of the innocent party in pursuing his rights.

## 17. No Partnership

*This agreement shall not be deemed to constitute an agency agreement or a partnership or joint venture or contract of employment between the parties.*

Clause 17 expressly provides that there is no partnership between the management and the artist (possibly the artist) and 18 confirms that English law will apply and the English courts have jurisdiction.

## 18. Governing Law

*This Agreement shall be governed and construed in accordance with the law of England and Wales the courts of which shall be courts of competent jurisdiction.*

In Chapter Three I have attempted to analyse the terms found in a standard form Management Agreement. Obviously the list of terms is not exhaustive, for such contracts are dynamic and are constantly being developed by music lawyers to suit the needs of their clients. Nevertheless I hope you will find that the fundamental terms of a management agreement have been examined and you can use this Chapter as a resource to provide guidance when negotiating drafting or interpreting a typical agreement. In Chapter Four, called Record Deals, and Chapter Five called Publishing Deals I have attempted to carry out a similar analysis in relation to a standard recording and publishing contract but by adopting a slightly different approach.

# Recording Contract Checklist

Chapter Four contains an analysis of a recording contract. Before a recording contract is signed the parties to it should be aware of the following:

* What is the contractual term and how long and often can the company extend it?

* Does the contract expire at the end of the initial term if the company fails to trigger an extension?

* On what grounds can the company suspend the contract and what are the consequences of the suspension?

* Is there any obligation on the record company to produce the master tapes and release and distribute the record?

* What are the consequences if the company fails to release or distribute?

* What is the product requirement during the contractual term?

  * album, singles, tracks, playing time? Can it be increased by the record company?

* Can the costs of an unsuccessful album as deemed advances be deducted for the royalties of a successful one?

* When are advances payable?

* What is the royalty rate and how often is it payable?

* What is the extent of copyright transferred and is it transferred for its full term?

* What is the recording schedule, is there a budget and is there room for negotiation over time and place?

* Who selects the material to be recorded and who chooses the products?

* Is the company committed to making and funding a promotional video, providing tour support and mounting an advertising campaign?

* What happens if a band member leaves? Can the company terminate the contract?

* Is a leaving band member bound to re-sign with the company as a solo artist?

* What happens to rights to recordings if the record company goes bust and is liquidated?

# Chapter Four
## Record Deals

Signing a record deal for a term of years is usually the most significant step in the career of an artist in the contemporary popular music industry. For the artist struggling for recognition it is the record deal that can put them on the ladder of success with the possibility of notoriety and fame. Understandably when the offer is made it is hard to resist. The potential rip off with overseas royalties doesn't seem so important when the record deal is on the table. This is particularly so when you consider how few bands get this far. Of course, like any contractual offer, it may be withdrawn prior to acceptance and a fresh offer made to another band elsewhere. An attempt to negotiate with a counter offer may be rejected by the record company and such a rejection will extinguish the original offer. The temptation then is to sign but as I've said before at you should know what you are letting yourself in for and the potential hazards.

## Artists Term Recording Contract

What do the parties provide each other under a standard term recording contract. Under the contract the creative artist (the band) will agree for a fixed term to perform services in accordance with a recording schedule to make singles and albums and transfer the copyright in the record material to the company, usually for the full period of the copyright.

In return the record company for a fixed term arranges the recording schedule and the promotional activities to market the product, pay advances to the artists, recoupable from royalties, and pays royalties to the artist based upon sales.

Recording contracts are adapted to suit the circumstances of the particular artist but generally an artist's term recording agreement will contain the following terms.

# The Contractual Terms

## 1.  The Parties

The contract will specify the date of the agreement and identify the parties. The record company will be named with the address of its registered office and the artist named with his address. If the artist is a band the individual names and addresses of all the members will be included. A reference is usually made that the band members jointly and severally constitute the artist and this we will see has important significance in relation to potential liability.

## 2.  Definitions

This is a crucial part of the contract and often overlooked, for it is only by appreciating the precise meaning of the words and phrases used in the contract that the parties can truly be said to be in agreement.

Obvious definitions that the parties should be aware of include what is meant by:

| | |
|---|---|
| *An album* | the number of tracks and playing time. |
| *The product* | the product required indicates the number of albums singles which should be made during the contractual term. |
| *Completion of recording* | this date often triggers the payment of advances. |

| | |
|---|---|
| *Distribution expenses/fees* | these could be relevant to an artist who is to receive a share of net profit from audio visual exploitation of the record. |
| *Initial period* | the contractual term without renewal. |
| *Option period* | company's right to extend the term usually tied to the product. |
| *Master tapes* | recordings of satisfactory artistic and technical quality. |
| *Recording costs* | company's own direct costs less overheads usually recoverable from artist's royalties payments. |
| *Territory* | this indicates the potential markets covered by the contract e.g. the UK, North America, the world, the solar system. |
| *Cross collateralisation* | the practice of deducting the costs of an unsuccessful album from the royalties of a successful one. |
| *Recording schedule* | timetable to produce the product which if agreed by negotiation is more likely to be adhered to. |
| *Recording budget* | genuine pre-estimate of the recording costs which the parties agree. |
| *Retail price* | this will determine the royalties paid to the artist and so the artist may seek to impose a minimum amount. |

| | |
|---|---|
| *Product requirement* | the precise number of albums and singles to be produced during the contractual term can be lengthened if the artist fails to maintain the product requirement or the contract is suspended. |
| *The services rendered by the artist* | the company will wish to ensure that they control the sole and exclusive services of the artist including the preparation, rehearsal, performance, writing, composing, arranging, designing, choreography and recording services of the artist in all audio and audio visual media and the promotional and publicity services of the artist. |

## 3.  Engagement

The definition section in a recording contract is followed by the substance of the agreement the contractual terms. Here the mutual rights and obligations of the recording company and the artist are included the company providing a list of model terms which may or may not be subject to negotiation. The precise nature of the services to be provided by the artist will be included with a requirement that they should be performed to the *best of the artist's ability in a professional and workmanlike manner and such time and locations that the company may from time to time require.*

Some artists could secure approval rights over *'times and locations'*. Some contracts provide that the *product requirement* could be unilaterally increased by the company and such a potential may be unacceptable to the artist. Certainly the selection of material to be recorded and in some cases the producer could be made matters over which the artist has exclusive control or at least approval rights.

The contract should identify what is required from the artist with regard to the recording sessions such as:

* attending adequate rehearsal sessions to ensure that studio time is not wasted
* co-operating with the producer and any musical arranger to ensure commercial quality
* attending recording sessions when required and repeating or re-recording material to ensure that the final version is of the best technical quality
* attending all mixing sessions to ensure that the final master is acceptable
* attending meetings to provide the information for the record sleeve and label and approve artwork and packaging
* co-operating in the production of promotional material including a video
* promoting the recorded material when giving live concerts and when on tour.

The contract should refer to the company's commitment to promoting the product through advertising, a video and providing tour support. The cost of producing a video could be recoverable from royalties or borne equally between the artist and the company.

Equally the contract will require a commitment for the artist to act professionally in the production of the product, to promote the product and retain his image including physical appearance.

In all contracts there is an express term providing that the company is under *no obligation to actually produce the Master Tapes or indeed release and distribute the records*. If the company insists on the inclusion of this clause it would be wise for the artist to extract an undertaking that the failure to release or distribute the product within a given period will result in a reversion of rights to the artist over the material, in other words the artist becomes the owner of the material. As there is potential liability on the company for failing to attempt to enhance the artist's reputation some contracts expressly exclude liability for this possibility. Such an exclusion clause may be resisted by the artist.

## 4.  Options

Here the contractual term is subject to multiple extensions at the option of the record company. There are often three option periods of the same length and often tied to a particular product requirement.

Surprisingly the contract may put the onus on the artist to serve written notice on the company about exercising its option to renew and giving the company a period to respond. Rather than fixed time periods, options could relate solely to the production of albums and singles but again this will usually stretch to a number of years.

Long term recording contracts which could, with the exercise of options, potentially last for seven or eight years may as we have seen be declared invalid as unreasonable restraints of trade.

In *ZTT v Holly Johnson* 1993 Dillon LJ declared that the *"on the general validity of the recording agreement, I find its provisions as to the duration of the term to be grossly one-sided"* and in the public interest the contract was unjustifiable as an unreasonable restraint of trade. Similarly in *Silvertone v Mountfield and Others* 1993 the Stone Roses recording contract was considered by the court and the fact that it could potentially last for a seven year term with the take up of a series of optional periods meant that the agreement was on policy grounds unenforceable as an unreasonable restraint of trade. Both the Stone Roses and the Holly Johnson contracts could have effectively prevented the artists from reaching the public over a considerable period bearing in mind the limited creative life of an artist in the popular music industry.

Why then did the High Court take a different view in the George Michael case in *1994 Panayiotou and Others v Sony Music Entertainment (UK) Ltd.* Despite the lengthy exclusive recording contracts the court was unsympathetic. Parker J felt that the option periods would be shortened if George Michael produced the albums more quickly and in any event they would only be taken up if the artist was successful and obtain substantial financial rewards. The fact that Michael was effectively shackled to Sony who were stifling his output was disregarded.

# 5. Grant of Rights

A number of terms will deal with the issue of copyright in the contract. Chapter One contains a brief outline of copyright law in relation to musical works. The record company will require the transfer of full world-wide copyright in the recorded product to be transferred for the full term of the copyright. The company will then have exclusive rights to grant licenses to manufacture, distribute and reproduce the product, for instance on a compilation album to exploit advertising and publicise the recording and to authorise public performance of the recording. The artist should not grant the exclusive right to use the band name to the company enabling the band to enter into endorsement contracts.

The transfer of world-wide copyright for its full term may be unacceptable to the artist. Unfortunately however the copyright position may be non negotiable. Merchandising rights however are negotiable and the artist may not wish to give then up to the company. It is important for the artist to retain the rights to exploit the artwork from the record sleeve and posters for merchandising purposes.

# 6.  Advances

A separate term will detail the company's undertaking to pay advances to the artist, usually on signing of the contract and then on completion of recording. Advances are of course recoupable from future royalties but they are not repayable if the releases are not commercially successful. Advances therefore represent an investment by the record company in the artist. The contract could provide that recording costs are deemed to be advances and they would be recoverable from royalties but only of course if the record is a commercial success. The artist should be made aware that he will bear such costs if the royalties can cover them. If aggregate advances are recoupable from aggregate royalties this means that the recording costs of an unsuccessful album can be recoverable from the royalties of a successful one. This called cross collateralisation and all recording artists should be made aware of it.

# 7.  Artists Warranties and Obligations

This term will provide in numerous clauses a list of undertakings made by the artist covering matters such as capacity of contract (see Chapter Two) confidentiality, union membership, health and professional name. As we discussed in Chapter Three there will be a specific clause confirming that the artist has sought and obtained legal advice before signing the contract. Inevitably artists obligations are usually company rights and one such right which may be of concern to an artist is the company right to *"use, adapt, change, revise, delete from, add to and/or rearrange the whole or any part of the product of the services and to combine the same with the whole or any part of any other work to any extent that the company shall desire"*. Such a wide discretion in relation to using the recorded material might be unacceptable to an established artist who wants to retain some control over her work and who may well insist on the inclusion of the expression *"with the artist's consent"* qualified by *"such consent not to be unreasonably withheld"*.

# 8.   Group Provisions

If the artist is a band then a number of provisions will be included to deal with potential liability, professional name, change of membership and leaving members. The recording contract is entered into by the company and the artist but if the artist is composed of a number of members then each member is individually contracted to the company. All of the obligations of the artist under the contract are joint and several which as we have already seen means that potentially one member could be sued individually for another's breach of contract.

This potential liability should be explained to the band and if it is unacceptable the contract should provide for that. Change of membership of the band is usually made subject to the written consent of the company following the service of a leaving notice. On the receipt of such notice the company has the option of terminating the recording contract. Usually the company will wish to reserve a sole and exclusive re-engagement option in relation to a leaving member. This would require a leaving member to sign with the company as a solo artist on similar terms and conditions. To be valid and enforceable such an option should be explained to band members before they sign the original contract. A further complication is that members of the band may not have equal status and the contract could identify key members who are given different treatment. If there are songwriters in the band they could be identified and the contract could provide that the band records there own compositions.

# 9.   Recording Restrictions

The contract will provide that during its term the artist can only perform and make recordings with the consent of the company. The company can consent to live recordings and all rights in such recordings will belong to the company. In addition the artist is restricted for a number of years from the end of the contract, usually five, from re-recording any of the material recorded during the term of the contract. This restriction would not apply to material not released during the terms or within 12 months of its termination.

## 10. Royalties

All royalties are made payable upon condition that the artist performs to obligations under the contract. They are calculated as a percentage of the royalty base price on net sales of albums inside the UK and a different percentage for sales outside the UK. The percentage will normally vary with the recording date from which the master tapes were derived rather than the release date. The percentage tends to increase following the initial periods to the first second and third option periods.

Most recording contracts have detailed royalty clauses and they require careful consideration. It is common to have different royalty rates for single, albums, and CDs, for the UK sales or sales in a designated territory and for sales outside the designated territory. Records distributed for promotional purposes will not attract a royalty and there could be concessionary rates and discounted rates for various purposes such as limited releases or supported by television advertising.

## 11. Royalty Accounting

Standard accounting clauses provide for six monthly statements of accounts indicating royalties due and accompanied by a payment of the amount. The artist will have the right to require that the accounts be audited once a year at his expense. If underpayment of royalties is revealed by the audit then the sum can be recovered plus interest and the costs in the audit met by the company. Artist's advances and where appropriate recording costs can be deducted for royalties and sometimes the contract will provide for deductions to meet potential tax liability provided a tax certificate is included.

# 12. Suspension and Termination

As previously mentioned the company will usually reserve the right to suspend the contract on the occurrence of a number of events such as:

* wilful refusal by the artist to perform contractual services
* breach of contract by the artist
* failing to submit to a medical examination for the purposes of insurance
* failing to perform services due to injury, illness, mental or physical disability
* force majeure preventing the company from making use of services or exploiting the records (see Chapter Three).

The effect of a suspension notice would be to extend the term and the recording schedule by the period of the suspension. Significantly for the artist during the period of suspension the company is relieved of its obligation to pay the artist.

The events which could lead to suspension could also give the company the right to terminate the contract. The service of a notice of termination will not affect the rights granted or assigned to the company under the contract (i.e. copyright) and the artist will only be entitled to payment of remuneration which accrued up to the date of termination.

So there you have it, a typical record deal. I am sure that you will appreciate that like management agreements, recording contracts are also dynamic and developed by lawyers on behalf of record companies and artists. My hope is that the standard terms that I have examined will nevertheless provide the parties to these contracts with food for thought. Certainly before an artist embarks on a relationship that could affect the rest of his life he should be advised to spend a little time in obtaining an appreciation of the significance of the deal on offer.

# Music Publishing Contract Checklist

Chapter Five contains an analysis of a composers term music publishing agreement. Before a publishing deal is signed the parties to it should be aware of the following:

* What is the term of the contract and how long can it be extended?

* Does the contract expire at the end of the initial term if the publisher fails to trigger an extension?

* Does the contract cover existing and future compositions?

* Is there an obligation on the publisher to publish the compositions?

* What extent of copyright is transferred to the publisher? Is it worldwide for its full term and can copyright revert to the composer?

* Can the publisher alter, adapt or add to the compositions?

* What is the writing commitment under the contract during the initial term and any option periods?

* In what circumstances can the contract be terminated or suspended by the publisher or the composer?

* Can the composer be required to compose for a third party?

* Can the composer engage a collaborator to assist in composing and does he have to sign a deal with the publisher?

* When a song is composed are the lyrics and the music treated as separate compositions?

* When do advances become payable under the contract?

* Where are royalties payable and what do they cover?

* How are joint compositions treated under the contract?

* Does the composer have to co-operate in promotional activities?

# Chapter Five
## Publishing Deals

Music publishing is one of the core activities in the popular music industry. EMI Music Publishing has the largest back catalogue in the world owning more than a million copyrighted songs. In May 1998 amid take-over speculation, EMI Music Publishing was valued at over a "cool billion pounds". Also it may not have escaped your attention that the leading cases in music contract law have arisen from the world of music publishing. The Tony Macaulay case on page 17 and the Fleetwood Mac decision on page 20 provide excellent guidance as to how the courts are prepared to scrutinise publishing contracts and in rare cases overturn them as oppressive contracts. Certainly music publishing is an integral part of the music business and it seems reasonable therefore in a book of this nature to devote some attention to exploring the content of a standard form publishing agreement. The aim of this chapter is to provide guidance to the young song writer about to commit himself to a publishing deal which could potentially extend through the most creative part of his career.

## Composer Term Music Publishing Agreement

This type of contract is used when a composer agrees to publish his material exclusively with a music publisher for a number of years. There are of course other types of publishing deals but I thought it would be most worthwhile to consider the content of a long term contract.

What do the parties provide each other under such contracts? Under the contract the composer will agree for a fixed term to perform services in accordance with an agreed schedule under which he will write compositions solely and exclusively for the publisher and usually transfer the entire copyright in the material to the publisher to hold for the full period of the copyright throughout the world.

In return the music publishing company, for a fixed term, produces and markets the product through its music catalogue, pays advances to the composers, recoupable from royalties, and pays royalties to the artist based upon sales.

Music publishing contracts are adapted to suit the circumstances of the particular artist but generally a standard publishing agreement will contain the following terms.

# The Contractual Terms

## 1.  The Parties

The contract will specify the date of the agreement and identify the parties. The publishing company will be named with the address of its registered office and the composer or composers named with their address. If the composers are members of a band, the band could be named but obviously the publishing deal relates to only the composer members.

## 2.  Definitions

This is a crucial part of the contract and often overlooked, for it is only by appreciating the precise meaning of the words and phrases used in the contract that the parties can truly be said to be in agreement.

Obvious definitions that the parties should be aware of include what is meant by:

| | |
|---|---|
| *Collaborator* | this is a person with whom the composer has collaborated in the writing of any of the compositions. |
| *Compositions* | this means existing compositions and also works partially completed during the contractual term which are referred to as future compositions. |
| *Cover record* | this means any commercial recording of a composition other than an original record. |
| *Initial period* | this means the original contractual term. |
| *Option period* | this means the publishers right to extend the term by exercising up to three options usually for one year at a time. |
| *Original record* | this means any commercial recording of a composition first made by the composer. |
| *Services* | this means the sole and exclusive services of the composer as a writer, composer, arranger and adapter of the works. |
| *Territory* | this indicates the potential markets covered by the contract e.g. the UK, North America, the world, the solar system. |
| *Works* | this means all musical compositions and lyrics, written, composed, orchestrated or arranged whether alone or in collaboration and stored by any method. The composer may wish to exclude certain works from the definition. |
| *Writing commitment* | the contract will indicate the number of compositions to be produced during the contractual term and during any future option periods. |

## 3.  Engagement

The definition section in a publishing contract is followed by the substance of the agreement, the contractual terms. Here the mutual rights and obligations of the publisher and the composer are included the publishing company providing a list of model terms which may or may not be subject to negotiation. The precise nature of the services to be supplied by the composer will be specified with a requirement that they should be performed to the best of the composers ability in a professional and workman like manner.

The composer will undertake to:

* write compositions solely and exclusively for the publisher;

* submit copies of all scores lyrics, vocal, instrumental and orchestral parts demo tapes, floppy discs, magnetic tapes and other means of recording or storing information relating to the compositions after they are written.

There could also be a requirement that the composer could be instructed to work under the direction of a third party to produce specific compositions. It may be that such a request is resisted by the composer. Also the contract may require the composer to engage in promotional activities but again such a provision may not be acceptable to the composer or indeed necessary.

## 4.  Options

Here the contractual term is subject to multiple extensions at the option of the publishing company. There are often three option periods usually of the same length (a year for each period).

Surprisingly the contract may put the onus on the composer to serve written notice on the publisher about exercising its option to renew and giving the company a period to respond. Long term publishing contracts which could, with the exercise of options, potentially last for seven or eight years may as we have seen be declared invalid as unreasonable restraints of trade. The leading case is still *Schroeder Music Publishing Co Ltd v Macaulay* 1974 a decision of the most senior court in England and Wales, the House of Lords. (See page 17)

## 5. Grant of Rights

A number of terms will deal with the issue of copyright in the compositions. In Chapter One you will remember there is a brief outline of copyright law in relation to musical works. The composer of a musical work is of course the original copyright owner and the contract will provide that the composer assigns (transfers) to the publisher the entire copyright in the compositions to hold for the full period of the copyright throughout the world. All the composers existing or future statutory rights relating to the compositions are also expressly waived in the contract. To enable the publisher to exploit the compositions the publisher will reserve the right to use the name likeness and biography of the composer for the full period of the copyright. The transfer of world-wide copyright for its full term may be unacceptable to the composer, however it should be stressed that the publisher may regard the copyright position as non negotiable.

## 6. Advances

A separate term will detail the company's undertaking to pay advances to the composer, usually on signing of the contract and then on fulfilling the writing commitment. Advances are of course recoupable from future royalties but like the recording contract, they are not repayable if the compositions are not commercially successful. Further advances are payable on the exercise of the publisher of the first and further option periods and the delivery of the writing commitment at the end of each option period.

## 7. Composers Warranties and Obligations

This term will provide in numerous clauses a list of undertakings made by the composer covering matters such as capacity of contract (see Chapter Two) confidentiality, membership of the Performing Rights Society, health and professional name. There will be a specific clause confirming that the composer has sought and obtained legal advice before signing the contract. The composer will undertake that the compositions are original and do not infringe any rights of copyright and confer on the publisher the complete control over the manner and extent of the exploitation of the compositions.

Both the publisher and the composer will be entitled to payments from the Performing Rights Society whenever the compositions are performed or played and the composers will undertake to co-operate by signing the division of fees form.

One undertaking that may be resisted by the composer is the authorisation to make alterations or adaptions of and additions to the compositions at the publishers discretion.

## 8. Publisher Obligations

While the composers obligations are quite extensive in a standard form publishing contract the publisher's obligations are usually succinct. The fundamental undertaking is to use all reasonable endeavours to procure the exploitation of the compositions whether by the publisher or any sub publisher.

# 9. Royalties

All royalties are made payable upon condition that the composer performs to obligations under the contract. They are calculated as a percentage of:

* the net sums distributed by the Performing Rights Society;

* the gross receipts from mechanical reproduction fees and sale of original records and cover records;

* the gross receipts from licensing of use of compositions;

* the retail selling price of each complete copy of the composition;

* a pro rata proportion of the percentage payable in respect of each copy of any publication containing the composition.

The composer will be entitled to a royalty in respect of a composition when it is performed, played, sold as a record, CD etc., included in a film play etc. or sold as sheet music. No fees or royalties are payable however in respect of copies of the composition given as complimentaries for promotional purposes.

# 10. Royalty Accounting

Standard accounting clauses provide for six monthly statements of accounts indicating royalties due and accompanied by a payment of the amount. The composer will have the right to require that the accounts be audited once a year at his expense. If underpayment of royalties is revealed by the audit then the sum can be recovered plus interest and the costs of the audit met by the publishing company.

# 11. Joint Compositions

If different composers are authors of the music and the lyrics then the contract can treat them as separate compositions and split the royalty accordingly. If new lyrics are added to existing music or vice versa then royalties again can be shared on an appropriate percentage. If the music and lyrics are composed by the same author it may still be worthwhile to treat them as separate compositions if they are likely to be exploited individually.

# 12. Collaboration

Any person who has assisted in the writing of the compositions is defined as a collaborator. The contract should specify that the composer should advise the collaborator that he is under an exclusive contract with the publisher. As a consequence the collaborator is required to grant to the publisher the same rights in any compositions produced as the composer grants under the contract. A proportion of the royalties is then payable to the collaborator in the proportion agreed with the composer. The term could also require that any notified collaborator should enter into a publishing deal with the music publisher.

# 13. Copyright Notices

The publisher will undertake to print the name of the composer on the cover or title page of every printed copy of the composition in accordance with the requirements of the Universal Copyright Convention and accord to the composer clear and legible credit as the author. This is an essential requirement for the composer to secure his rights in certain countries.

# 14. Suspension and Termination

The publisher will usually reserve the right to suspend the contract on the occurrence of a number of events such as:

* wilful refusal by the artist to perform contractual services

* breach of contract by the artist

* failing to submit to a medical examination for the purposes of insurance

* failing to perform services due to injury, illness, mental or physical disability

* force majeure preventing the company from making use of services or exploiting the records (see Chapter Three).

The effect of a suspension notice would be to extend the term by the period of the suspension. Significantly for the composer during the period of suspension the company is relieved of its obligation to pay the composer.

The events which could lead to suspension could also give the company the right to terminate the contract. The service of a notice of termination will not affect the rights granted or assigned to the company under the contract (i.e. copyright) and the artist will only be entitled to payment of remuneration which accrued up to the date of termination.

Termination by a composer is also provided for in a standard contract when there has been material default by the publisher or the publisher's liquidation. Such a termination requires written notice with an opportunity for the publisher to remedy the default. In the event of termination by the composer all rights in future compositions revert to the composer.

I explained at the beginning of the Chapter that in this type of publishing contract the Publishing House is investing in the talent of the songwriter for a number of years. For this reason such contracts should only be signed after obtaining legal advice and then reflecting on what is on offer. Hopefully this book goes a little way in clearing a path through the legal maze. I suppose that without the legal maze there would be less need for lawyers or even law teachers like myself. Such a thought is of course like the unlikely possibility of Newcastle United's demise, too horrible to even contemplate.

# Index

## A

Accept a repudiation 39, 72, 79

Accountants 59

Accounting 75, 76

Advances 54, 74, 85, 94
  aggregate advances 94
  aggregate royalties 94

Agent 8, 76

Album 82, 88

Appointment 57

Approval Rights 91

Arranging 90

Joan Armatrading 9, 38

Artwork 93

Assignment 79

Audio Visual Media 90

Audit 96, 107

Author 108

## B

Band Name 68, 71, 95

Gary Barlow 72

Barron Knights 43

Beatles 6

Ed Bicknell 6, 7, 24

## B (continued)

Breach of Contract 9, 44, 45, 71, 72, 79, 97, 109

Business Property 14

David Bryce 6

## C

Cassettes 14

Caveat Emptor 16

Choreography 90

Eric Clapton 6

Collaborator 99, 103

Collaboration 108

Commercial Recording 103

Commission 6, 12, 37, 38, 49, 55, 63, 74, 75 75

Compilation 93

Composer 99, 107

Composing 90

Compositions 98, 99, 103, 106

Conditions 39

Confidentiality Clause 64, 94, 106

Conflict of Interest 71

Consumer Credit Act 7

Contempt of Court 10

Contract

  accept a repudiation 72

  breach 9, 44-46, 71, 79, 109

  consideration 30, 31

  counter offer 30

  of employment 12, 26, 36

  express terms 57

  frustration 42, 43

  hire purchase 13

  implied terms 40

  intended legal relations 7

  mistake 34

  performance 41

  standard form contract 19, 21

  terms 38-40

  uberrimae fidei 31

  written contract 11-13, 26

Consensus ad idem 22 32

Consumer Credit Act 13

Contractual term 38-40

Copyright 13-15, 18, 85, 87, 93, 99

  convention 108

  derivative works 14

  designing 14

  mixing 14

  musical work 13

  patent 14

  typographical arrangements 14

  typesetting 14

Cover Record 103

Copyright Designs and Patents Act 1988 13, 76

Cross collateralisation 89, 94

**D**

Damages 9, 33, 44, 45

Ray Davies 9

Definitions and Interpretations 53, 88, 102

Lord Denning 6

Distribution 23, 89

Double employment rule 52

Duress 35

**E**

Earnings 54

Employment Agency 60, 63

Engagement Agreements 55, 57, 59, 66, 73

EMI 9, 101

Employment Agencies Act 1973 60, 63

Endorsement Contracts 93

Entertainment Industry 53

European Court 16

Expenses 55, 74

Express Terms 57

  options 57

  suspension 57

  termination 57

**F**

Fiduciary Duty 35, 52, 72, 75, 76, 77

Film 53

Fines 11

Fixed Term 102

Fleetwood Mac 20, 101

Floppy Discs 104

Force Majeure 44, 56, 57, 58, 97

Roger Forrester 6

Fraud 16, 32

Freedom of Contract 15, 16

Frustration 57, 42, 43

**G**

Genesis 6

Gross Income 55, 56, 73, 74

Gross Receipts 107

Guns N' Roses 44

**H**

Health 67, 106

High Court 9, 11, 16

House of Lords 17, 105

Whitney Houston 10

**I**

In Kind 56

Indemnify 68, 69

Independent 32

Initial Period 103

Injunction 45

Implied Terms 40

Insurance 78, 80

Intend Legal Relations 7

**J**

Ray Jackson 9

Elton John 9

Holly Johnson 9, 19, 92

Joint Compositions

Joint and Several 51, 70, 95

**K**

Key Member 48, 51, 72, 95

Kinks 6

Allen Klein 6

Mark Knopfler 6, 7

**L**

Leaving Member 71, 95

Leaving Notice 71

Legal Advice 10, 13, 20, 54, 68

Legal Liability 8, 9

Legal Sanctions 11

Licenses 63, 107

Lindisfarne 9

Live Recordings 95

Lyrics 99, 108

**M**

Tony Macaulay 17, 18, 101

Magnetic Tapes 104

Management 13

Management Agreement 26, 82

Management Services 62

Manufacturing 23

Nigel Martin-Smith 10, 21, 71, 72, 75

Master Tapes 82, 89, 91

Paul McCartney 9

Christine McVie 20

Mechanical Reproductions 107

Merchandising 23, 25, 93

George Michael 9, 10, 16, 37, 93

Minor 31, 37

Misrepresentation 16, 23, 33

Mixing 91

Mobility Clauses 27

Model Terms 104

Mortgage 8

Musical Rights 76

Musical Works 13

## N

Net Profit 89

North America 58, 89, 103

Notice of Termination 79

## O

Offer and Acceptance 26, 28-30

Options 61, 62, 89, 92, 103, 104

Oral Contract 11, 26

Original Record 103

Hazel O'Connor 42

Jason Orange 72

Orchestrated 104

Gilbert O'Sullivan 19, 20

## P

Larry Page 22

Partnership 70, 82

Performing Rights Society 106, 107

Personal Appearance 54, 67

Pink Floyd 6

Power of Attorney 58

Precedents 13

Prince 8

Product Endorsement 61

Product Requirement 82, 88, 90

Professional Name 68, 71, 95

Promotes 8, 36

Public Policy 15

Publisher 13, 17, 18, 99

Publishing 20, 21, 27, 77, 98-110

Publishing House 110

## R

Recording 23, 25

Recording
  budget 89
  costs 89
  company 13, 17,
  deal 20, 21, 28, 82, 83, 87-98
  restrictions 95
  schedule 85, 89
  sessions 91
Registered Address 51
Rehearsal 90
Rehearsal Sessions 91
Release 82
Repudiation 79
Restraint of Trade 17-19, 35-38, 92
Retail Selling Price 107
Retail Price 89
Cliff Richard 6
Royalties 14, 54, 85, 87, 91, 94, 96

**S**

Sale of Goods Act 7
Services 103
Sheet Music 107
Single 82, 87
Tony Smith 6
Solo Artist 85
Song 9
Phil Spector 15
Specific Performance 46

Sponsorship 23, 53, 61
Standard Form Contract 19, 21
Stone Roses 19, 92
Subject to Contract 63
Substantial Performance 41-42
Suspension 77, 78, 97, 109
Suspension Notice 109

**T**

Take That 12, 24, 26, 63, 64, 69, 71, 72, 75
Tax Certificate 96
Television 53
Television Advertising 96
Territory 55, 60, 89, 103
Termination 78, 79, 97, 109
Times and Locations 90
Touring 23, 91
Tour Manager 54
Tour Support 56, 91
Pete Townshend 5
Tracks 82, 88
Training 67
Troggs 22

**U**

Uberrimae Fidei 33
Undue Influence 19, 20, 35
Union Membership 65, 94
Universal Copyright Convention 108
Unliquidated Damages 44

# V

Vaudeville 53

Video 85, 91

Void 29, 81

Voidable 32

# W

Waiver 81

Warner Bros 8, 15

Warranties 39, 69, 70, 94

The Who 6

Robbie Williams 10, 21, 24,
  52, 63, 64, 71, 72

Works 103

Writing Commitment 103

Written Agreement 7, 11-13

# Other Titles from Harrison Law Publishing

Employment Law 3rd Edition ISBN 0907679-99-4     £16.95

Business Law 4th Edition ISBN 0907679-92-7     £19.95

Business Law GNVQ Advanced Level 3
ISBN 0907679-55-2     £12.95